Plutocratic Socialism

Plutocratic Socialism

The Future of Private Property and the Fate of the Middle Class

by

Mark T. Mitchell

Front Porch Republic *Books*

PLUTOCRATIC SOCIALISM
The Future of Private Property and the Fate of the Middle Class

Front Porch Republic Books
An Imprint of Wipf and Stock Publishers
199 W. 8th Ave., Suite 3
Eugene, OR 97401

www.wipfandstock.com

PAPERBACK ISBN: 978-1-6667-3658-8
HARDCOVER ISBN: 978-1-6667-9511-0
EBOOK ISBN: 978-1-6667-9512-7

VERSION NUMBER 042622

To Seth, Noah, Scott, and Tana.
May you feel both the gratitude of your inheritance
as well as the burden of its responsibility.

In America there are no proletarians.

—ALEXIS DE TOCQUEVILLE

Rage and phrenzy will pull down more in half an hour,
than prudence, deliberation, and foresight can build up
in a hundred years.

—EDMUND BURKE

Theologians talk about a prevenient grace that precedes grace
itself and allows us to accept it. I think there must also be
a prevenient courage that allows us to be brave—that is, to
acknowledge that there is more beauty than our eyes can bear,
that precious things have been put into our hands and to do
nothing to honor them is to do great harm. And therefore, this
courage allows us, as the old men said, to make ourselves
useful. It allows us to be generous, which is another way
of saying exactly the same thing.

—MARILYNNE ROBINSON

Contents

Preface: Plutocratic Socialism and the Corruption of Democracy | ix

Introduction: Plutocratic Socialism Comes to America | 1

CHAPTER ONE
Private Property: An Enduring Concept | 17

CHAPTER TWO
Property From Jamestown to Philadelphia | 32

CHAPTER THREE
A Republic, If You Can Keep it | 47

CHAPTER FOUR
Challenges to Property: Revolutions Political and Industrial | 61

CHAPTER FIVE
Men at Work: Stewards in a Ragtag Garden | 74

CHAPTER SIX
Plutocrats, Socialists, and American Politics | 90

CHAPTER SEVEN
Virtue and Citizenship: How Property Makes Citizenship Possible | 103

CHAPTER EIGHT
Privacy and Stewardship: Restoring Lost Ideals | 115

CHAPTER NINE
Conclusion: Renewing Property to Renew America | 130

Afterword: Building a Multiracial Middle-Class Coalition | 146

Acknowledgements | 155
Bibliography | 157
Index | 163

Plutocratic Socialism
and the Corruption of Democracy

It is the crisis of the middle class, and not simply the growing chasm between wealth and poverty, that needs to be emphasized in a sober analysis of our prospects.

—CHRISTOPHER LASCH

ANYONE WHO STUDIES POLITICS must keep one vital principle in mind: power tends to expand and consolidate. If you lose sight of that fact, everything else will go out of focus. Political thinkers have long understood this axiom of power. James Madison, writing in *The Federalist Papers*, put the matter succinctly: "power is of an encroaching nature." In light of this fact, he set out to describe the principle of separation of powers built into the United States Constitution. Of course, the underlying assumption is clear: consolidated power is dangerous and undesirable. When power is sufficiently consolidated, the practical consequence is tyranny.

That having been said, any adequate conception of politics requires sufficient power to make collective action possible. If power is absolutely diffuse, political institutions cannot function. If it is absolutely unified, politics will die. Power, then, is necessary but dangerous. Human communities require it but must at the same time constantly guard against power's natural tendency to unify and grow.

Institutional structures can provide some measure of protection. The U.S. Constitution delegates specific powers to the three branches with the hope that those branches will jealously guard their power against the inevitable encroachments of the others. They "check" each other. The federal structure of our government is also intended to provide the same insurance: the states are tasked with checking the expansion of the national government. However, these sorts of institutional checks are no guarantee. In fact, it is likely that they will fail if two other conditions do not exist. First, Madison admitted that "a dependence of the people is, no doubt, the primary control on the government." By this he meant that virtuous and vigilant citizens are the best means of checking the expansion of power. The second condition is a vibrant middle class characterized by the ownership of private property. These two ideals are related, for the ownership of property calls forth certain virtues that make self-government possible. The virtues of self-control, independence, generosity, thrift, and neighborliness are fostered, at least in part, by a culture of private property. Ultimately, the Founders understood something that we, too, must grasp: property and power are inseparable.

Our constitutional order assumes a populace of property owners, a middle class whose virtues provide the necessary ballast to support our republic. Our founders imagined strong communities, strong families, and independent citizens capable of self-government. They knew if the people degenerate into an insolent plutocracy on the one hand and a disgruntled, insecure, proletarianized mass on the other, the American experiment in self-government would become increasingly fragile and eventually collapse.

This unraveling is happening before our eyes. A plutocracy—that is, rule by the wealthy and their surrogates—is emerging as large public and private entities exercise increasing power through both the law and the market. This is characterized by an incestuous union of Big Government and Big Business, neither of which has the interests of the citizen-consumer in mind. As I write, the government is expanding its reach to compel citizens to submit to an array of mandates including Covid protocols, racially charged educational curricula, climate-change standards, pervasive surveillance, and militarized police forces, all ostensibly justified by our fears. At the same time, corporations wield their power by aggressively promoting a radical social agenda and in the process depriving consumers of such basic goods as privacy or a platform for free speech. Employees who don't toe the line retreat into fearful silence or lose their jobs. As the wealth gap grows, insecure citizens clamor for economic security via government programs, subsidies, and guarantees. Political and economic insecurity provides the opportunity for the plutocrats to entrench their power by means of handouts that only temporarily mask the underlying problems. Trillions in deficit spending assuage present demands at the expense of future freedom. Indeed, we are exchanging the freedom of our descendants for the illusion of security today. They will be justified in destroying the statues we erect to honor ourselves.

Yet wealth is not sufficient for gaining access to the current plutocratic class. What is also necessary is a particular outlook, a plutocratic psychology, if you will. This illusory meritocracy is rooted in the false belief that wealth, or proximity to wealth, is an indication of special moral virtue. Not surprisingly, this belief manifests itself in a disposition of self-righteousness whereby those infected by it come to see themselves as superior to their fellow-citizens who are, alas, not wealthy or connected. They come to see themselves as above the law, for law is necessary for controlling the common citizen, but it is certainly not something that should limit those possessing the moral superiority that wealth would seem to denote. Thus, the plutocracy in America today is characterized by both insolence and self-righteousness, and it is not conveniently confined to either the Left or Right.

I must emphasize here that this is not a polemic against wealth or an argument seeking to justify the state-sponsored reallocation of wealth in the service of some utopian vision of equality. Wealth is not the problem. Any society where citizens are free to buy, sell, and to own and dispose of their property will result in inequalities. Christ told us that the poor would always be among us. So too the wealthy. The problem I am addressing is a particular view that claims a connection between wealth and moral virtue and a political structure that privileges the wealthy over everyone else. There is a world of difference between a society consisting of a majority of citizens who are middle class and who exercise a controlling influence over the political landscape and a society consisting of a shrinking middle class and growing wealth disparities. In such a situation, the wealthy will invariably possess power disproportionate to their virtue. America today is confronted by this unhealthy social and political situation.

A plutocratic class, if it is to survive in a democratic age, must placate insecure, propertyless citizens with state-sponsored benefits that provide the illusion of security. This welfare state will, in time, generate explicit calls for socialist policies and programs. Plutocratic Socialism, then, is a system built on a symbiotic relationship between two seemingly opposed classes: plutocrats and socialists. We are now witnessing this in America. Moreover, the newest iteration of socialism today has joined with the regnant social justice movement creating a toxic brew of social, political and economic pathologies—call it Woke Socialism.

It is important to appreciate the fundamental tension inherent in the union of plutocracy and woke socialism. Woke socialism is rooted in the claim that the world is sharply divided between two classes construed in various ways as the oppressors and the oppressed, the victimizers and the victims, the powerful and the weak. Plutocrats clearly hold the power and those deemed oppressed or marginalized—people of color, women, the poor, those identifying as LGBT, etc.—do not. It is at this point that things get dicey. Plutocrats must appear to make common cause with the oppressed lest they forfeit the perception of moral authority. To do so they must either 1) engage in a cynical charade where they merely pretend to uphold the cause of the oppressed, 2) enter into a deeply conflicted position where a sense of guilt induces acts and words of sympathy for the oppressed all while desperately clinging to the wealth, status, and power that seems to implicate them as oppressors, or 3) convince themselves that their special virtue and status provide them with the unique opportunity to do important work on behalf of the oppressed thereby legitimating their own relentless hold on wealth, status, and power. In short, they must either descend into abject hypocrisy, succumb to the psychic turmoil rooted in self-hatred, or delude themselves with a vision of their own moral superiority and indispensability. The perilous nature of these gambits is glaring.

Some have taken to using the term "woke capitalism" to describe this dynamic, but that does not accurately capture the reality of our moment. We must distinguish between woke capital, which surely exists, and woke capitalism, the existence of which is less obvious. Today corporate, cultural, and political elites harass those who do not bow to the woke agenda. They combine their power to enforce the compliance of private individuals and businesses and to bully local and state officials. The problem, then, is not capitalism run amok. Instead powerful elites use private capital and political positions to 1) leverage government, corporate, and cultural power to compel compliance with the woke agenda, and 2) they champion policies and direct public resources to placate the demands of the populace that is haunted by economic and social insecurity. The incestuous relationship between public and private power indicates the presence of something far different from a free market of goods, services, and ideas.

The combination of plutocracy and insecure, aggrieved citizens can also produce the conditions for revolution. Glaring abuses of power, inequalities widely deemed unjust, and a citizenry deeply distrustful of basic institutions are lethal ingredients and seem to justify those clamoring to dismantle the system by, among other things, abolishing private property and thereby destroying free market capitalism, both of which are seen as primary impediments to a better world.

There exists, then, a natural continuum from an ever-expanding welfare state to the abolition of private property. We might call it "the socialist continuum." Once aggressive welfare policies are implemented (as opposed to a modest and limited social safety net), the sacred idea of property will gradually dissipate. Confiscation and redistribution undermine the status of property and kindle dreams of a world without private property. After all, if property is the most prominent and concrete expression of inequality, and if inequality is seen as synonymous with injustice, one can presumably eliminate inequality—and injustice—by eliminating property.

Although our current plutocratic class pays lip service to democracy, self-reliance, and liberty, the rhetoric hides the reality where fear, economic insecurity, and petulant demands for autonomy foster the conditions of dependence. The plutocracy naturally favors the welfare state, for it is an effective means of both pacifying insecure citizens and fostering the illusion of plutocratic virtue. However, when the people are organized and radicalized, they can seek to push the logic to its natural end, namely, the total transformation of society and the transformation of property, which if successful, would destroy the plutocracy. Thus, the plutocrats will anxiously dole out enough baubles to keep the citizens distracted, enough services to blunt the despair, and enough fear-mongering to keep them cowering all in an effort to prevent the socialist continuum from playing out to its logical conclusion. Socialist leaders will, in the process, find ways to gain personal advantage from the immense flood of resources pouring in their direction.

Plutocratic Socialism, then, represents a strange alliance that would have stunned and dismayed Marx. It is as if the bourgeoisie and the proletariat decided to strike a secret pact and work together rather than allow their rancorous animosity to ignite a full-blown revolution. The leadership of both classes have much to gain by this seemingly bizarre arrangement. Plutocrats gain moral legitimacy, and socialists gain wealth, status, and power, ironically the very things cherished by the plutocrats. Perhaps this hidden dynamic is one reason why socialist revolutions rarely, if ever, come to a successful termination but instead remain stuck in a "transitional" phase where the plutocrats—and those fortunate individuals drawn into their orbit—secure the wealth, status, and power while the revolutionary energy of the masses is allowed to burn out in frustration.

There is another way. A broad middle class, characterized by the ownership of private property, is the only real means by which citizens possess both the power to govern themselves and the virtues necessary to do so. This suggests a crucial insight: if wealth is unduly concentrated, power will be unduly concentrated as well. The inverse is also true. If property is broadly owned, power will be broadly distributed. The latter ideal is the essence of a healthy democracy.

Many utopian schemers today imagine a world where the inconvenience of private property is but an unpleasant memory and where technocratic wizards make life safe, pleasant, and worry-free for everyone as long as they submit to the "reasonable" standards of the elites. These self-righteous planners see property, at least for everyone other than themselves, as a source of unrest, inequality, and injustice. However, a plutocratic socialism energized by a woke agenda of race ideology and climate hysteria is not a path to liberation but to certain degradation and bondage.

Today we stand at a crucial moment in our nation's history, and our actions will determine our collective fate. We can choose dependency and servitude at the hands of our plutocratic masters or we can choose the freedom that is inseparable from a society shaped by the ownership of private property. The first step is, as always, to see clearly. We must recognize the basic facts of our condition if we hope to have any chance of providing a remedy. Our analysis must begin with a simple, yet profound, axiom: private property and political freedom stand or fall together.

Introduction

Plutocratic Socialism Comes to America

The government of democracy is the only one in which he who
votes the tax can escape the obligation to pay it.

—ALEXIS DE TOCQUEVILLE

IN A 2019 GALLUP Poll, 43 percent of Americans claimed that some form
of socialism would be good for the country. The same question was put
to Americans in 1942, during the grim days of WWII. Then only 25 percent had a favorable view of socialism. Today Americans who identify
with the Democratic Party have a more positive view of socialism than
of capitalism. When asked about the future of governments globally, in
1949 72 percent of respondents believed that most nations would have a
democratic form of government while, only 14 percent believed that the
future would be socialist. In 2019 57 percent believed the future would
be democratic, while 29 percent believed that socialism would prevail.[1]
Events such as the housing crisis of 2008 and the pandemic of 2020
served to accelerate dramatically the trend toward socialist policies.

What happened? How could America, the land of the free, a nation that played a decisive role in defeating both National Socialism and
Communism, come to embrace a version of the very ideology that it so
confidently opposed for the greater part of the twentieth century? Or,
more accurately, how could nearly half of Americans come to this conclusion? Of course, in this 2019 poll 51 percent of Americans claimed
socialism is a bad thing, and it might be safe to conclude that this stark

1. Younis, "4 in Ten Americans."

1

division is one inflection point in the rancorous divisions rending the political and social fabric of our nation today.

One of the factors helping to energize this new enthusiasm for socialism is the perception that the middle class is shrinking while the poor and wealthy are both expanding. A 2020 Pew Research Center report found "a steep fall in the share of U.S. aggregate income held by the middle class." The data indicate that from 1970 to 2018 "the share of aggregate income going to middle-class households fell from 62% to 43%."[2] A report published by the Economic Policy Institute found that between 1945 and 1973 "the top 1 percent captured just 4.9 percent of all income growth over that period." However, between 1973 and 2007 the trend dramatically reversed: "58.7 percent of all income growth [was] concentrated in the hands of the top 1 percent of families."[3]

New leaders in the Democratic Party, people who call themselves "progressives," are at the forefront of this surging popularity of socialism, and this is pulling the party as a whole to favor policies that not long ago no mainstream Democrat could have safely embraced. The so-called Green New Deal, introduced into the House of Representatives in 2019 by freshman firebrand Alexandra Ocasio-Cortez, proposed massive amounts of spending to counter the effects of climate change and to reverse a wide array of social and economic inequalities and insecurities—referred to generally as "systemic injustices"—that disproportionately effect "frontline and vulnerable communities." The connection between these various afflictions? They are all ostensibly caused by capitalism.

The Green New Deal has come to symbolize the aspirations of a new "woke" Socialism, a movement motivated by 1) fear that a changing climate threatens the future of humanity, 2) insecurity produced by power held disproportionately by corporations and white men, and 3) the conviction that inequalities—both social and economic—are unjust, harmful, and need to be rectified. To achieve these goals, the Green New Deal proposes "a new national, social, industrial, and economic mobilization on a scale not seen since World War II and the New Deal era."[4]

The presidential candidacy of Bernie Sanders in 2016 and 2020 helped bring socialism into the mainstream. Then in 2020 financial difficulties associated with the coronavirus pandemic drove millions

---

2. Horowitz, Igielnik and Kochhar, "Trends in income and wealth inequality."
3. Sommeiller and Price, "The New Gilded Age."
4. United States Congress (116th), H. Res. 109.

to look to the federal government for relief. Unemployment, housing foreclosures, failed businesses, and a profound sense of insecurity all contributed to a general sense that the system is deeply flawed. The federal government sent out cash payments to millions of citizens. Some demanded the suspension of mortgage and rent payments along with a guaranteed income. Businesses received federal money to stay solvent. No one knew how much would suffice, but virtually everyone seemed to agree that the proper role of the federal government was to provide relief regardless of the cost.

Many progressives saw the coronavirus as an opportunity. House Majority Whip Jim Clyburn recognized the potential of the crisis, noting that it provided a "tremendous opportunity to restructure things to fit our vision."[5] Alexandra Ocasio-Cortez remarked that she was "thankful" that the coronavirus helped people to see the "fragility of our system."[6] Joe Biden also recognized the possibilities: "Every great change that has taken place has come out of a crisis. . . . And I think we have an opportunity now to significantly change the mindset of the American people, things they weren't ready to do."[7] The transformation of American society seemed to be possible, and socialism was no longer a dirty word. In fact, for many caught up in the chaos of the coronavirus response, socialism seemed not only plausible but desirable.

Significant incursions of the federal government into the market found support among a majority of Americans, not just liberals and progressives. In April 2020, during the spring coronavirus lockdown, a poll found that 74 percent of Republicans and 84 percent of Democrats favored moving to a universal health care system. 76 percent said that people who contracted Covid-19 should not be charged for medical costs. 82 percent claimed that a one-time stimulus check was inadequate. 55 percent said that mortgage and rent payments should be frozen, and 63 percent claimed private student loan payments should be suspended.[8] The level of insecurity was profound, and the federal government seemed the only reasonable shelter and source of relief.

Then on May 25, 2020, in Minneapolis, George Floyd, an African-American man, died after an arresting officer subdued him with a knee

---

5. Stewart, "Rep. Jim Clyburn Has Been Here Before."

6. Herndon, "Alexandra Ocasio-Cortez has Never Spoken to Joe Biden."

7. Matamoros, "Sanders: Rethinking."

8. Onepoll, "Covid-19 Has Changed Americans' Opinions."

pressed to the neck for more than eight minutes. The agonizing video showed Floyd begging the officer to let him breath. "I can't breathe" became the battle cry of protestors expressing rage about police violence directed at blacks. The protests quickly turned violent and spread to cities around the nation. The call for justice transformed into a violent assault against a system that was ostensibly responsible not only for the death of George Floyd but for the misery and inequality of all those lacking "privilege."

Businesses were looted and burned. Demands for economic justice were indiscriminately mingled with theft and destruction of property. The logic, implied in the actions, seemed to be something like this: "I have been deprived of material goods and economic opportunities by a system that is fundamentally corrupt. Thus, stealing and destroying property that has been unjustly acquired is not unjust but rather a vigorous step toward overturning a rotten system." If property represents power, then the destruction of property would seem to represent the destruction of that power. At the same time, this line of argument gave rise to the claim that looting was merely a form of reparations for past racial injustices.[9]

In the rage to destroy the system, the logic of climate change met an unexpected ally, social justice. For years the climate warriors had been warning that the earth was under assault and that time was short. We were nearing a point of no return when the rising temperatures would be irreversible and world-wide death and destruction would ensue. Journalist and climate writer Paul Mason insisted that "to save the planet, we have to end capitalism," and unless we act swiftly, we face "global catastrophe."[10] The language of crisis has become commonplace among those concerned about the climate. This same sense of crisis grew acute as the coronavirus lock-downs of 2020 persisted. With unemployment topping 40 million, the fear and insecurity were profound. The killing of George Floyd was a match to the powder keg of resentment, anxiety, and frustration. It also provided an opportunity for the cultural nihilists to capitalize on the protests. The common culprit responsible for the death of George Floyd, social and economic inequalities, racism, the patriarchy, and climate change: white, capitalist power structures. The antiracist guru Ibram X. Kendi put the matter succinctly and with his characteristic antipathy to nuance: "Capitalism is essentially racist; racism is essentially

9. Fitz-Gibbon, "Black Lives Matter Organizer Calls Chicago Looting 'Reparations.'" See also Osterweil, *In Defense of Looting*.

10. Mason, "My Manifesto for a Post-Carbon Future."

capitalist."[11] This system, we are told, must be dismantled and replaced with something more just. The alternative: Woke Socialism. But a peaceful transformation was by no means inevitable. In a poll taken less than three weeks after the death of Floyd, 42 percent of likely voters said they believed the U.S. would likely or very likely experience a second civil war in the next five years.[12]

It is important to point out that the term "socialism" has become a catch-all term that means various things to different people. "Communism" is sometimes used interchangeably with "socialism." Both terms are used to describe an economic system and also a political and social vision. Those who have absorbed their Marx will recall that he insisted that his theory "could be summed up in a single sentence: Abolition of Private Property." This would include a move "to centralise all instruments of production in the hands of the State." He admitted that the initial phase of the revolution would require "despotic inroads on the rights of property," including the "abolition of property in land," "a heavy progressive or graduated income tax," "the abolition of the right of inheritance," the "confiscation of the property of all emigrants and rebels," the "centralization of credit in the hands of the State," and the "centralization of the means of communication and transport in the hands of the State."[13] Yet this revolutionary transformation of property would be a small price to pay for the equality, justice, and happiness that would result.

Some who are accused of championing socialism are interested primarily in fixing the current economic system by working to reduce income inequality and improving the conditions of workers. The expansion of the welfare state is their primary goal; however, given the socialist continuum, the abolition of property and a continually expanding welfare state share a common essence. The Woke Socialists, of course, make no effort to disguise their intent in the rhetoric of an old-fashioned welfare state. They are much more ambitious. They are concerned with "systemic" inequality and "systemic" injustice and believe that the current system is fundamentally flawed and must be abandoned. But where Marx argued that the evil of capitalism was found in the perpetuation of a capitalist economic class and the oppression of the working class,

11. Kendi, *How to be an Antiracist*, 163.
12. *Rasmussen Report*, "31% Think U.S. Civil War Likely Soon."
13. Marx, *The Marx-Engels Reader*, 484, 490.

the Woke Socialist agenda takes on the mantle of the social justice warriors who see systemic injustices not simply in economic terms but in the very DNA of what they see as our white, patriarchal, cisgender power structures.[14] Thus, while Marx saw world history through the lens of class struggle, these neo-Marxists see the world through the tri-focal lens of race, class, and gender. Where Marx's revolutionary vision centered on the ascendance of the proletariat class and the demise of the bourgeois class and its institutions, the revolutionary vision of the Woke Socialists goes beyond economics to include total transformation propelled by the engine of identity politics. Nature, itself, becomes a target for transformation as biological realities are denied and technological "advances" amplify the power of the revolution. This is a Marxist revolution on steroids.

The Green New Deal and similar proposals sought to bring about revolutionary change through a political process. The waves of violent protests precipitated by the death of George Floyd seemed intended to dismantle the system by violence and chaos. Though their tactics differed, both sides employed the rhetoric of revolution, directed their hostility toward—among other things—capitalism, and expressed their desire for a more just and equitable system. Their apparent aim was to replace the current system—characterized by systemic injustice and irreparable pathologies—with something vaguely termed "socialism."

To be sure, this new breed of Socialist correctly intuits that something is amiss. Ideas, it is true, have consequences. They also have antecedents. There are social forces predating the coronavirus that helped pave the way for this new resurgence of socialism, and we do well to consider some of the most significant.

It is hard to miss the prevailing sense of insecurity and general angst that characterize our present moment. There are, to be sure, the optimistic techno-utopians who breezily assure us that whatever problems we encounter will be overcome by the wizardry of our technological innovations. There are the purveyors of information and abstraction who have experienced dizzying levels of profits in recent years and fail to recognize that their feeling of insulation against the hard edges of reality is not shared by the vast majority, whose fortunes have flagged during the same years. Despite these anomalous individuals and groups, most Americans sense that the stability for which we all long is breaking apart. We have come to wonder what, if anything, binds us together as fellow citizens.

14. See, for instance, Hannah-Jones et al., "The 1619 Project."

Many have come to wonder if the centrifugal forces at work in our society have become irresistible. If things are coming apart, perhaps the fault is a corrupt system. If the system can be replaced, perhaps we can finally achieve the solidarity that characterizes a just society.

The sources of this anxiety are legion and were only exacerbated by the coronavirus pandemic of 2020. Unemployment, isolation, and fear of illness all contributed to a foreboding sense of dread. However, even prior to the rise of the coronavirus, growing income inequality, along with declining social mobility, led some to conclude we are entering into a new feudal age.[15] The cost of higher education has skyrocketed along with the growing perception that a college diploma (or even a graduate degree) is a necessary ticket to success (and therefore happiness). As a result, Americans are incurring massive amounts of student debt that, ironically, limits their options after graduation (and therefore diminishes their happiness). We hear of dramatic increases in the number of college graduates moving back in with their parents because job prospects are dismal and the debt is overwhelming. We hear of young men who wile away their lives playing video games, inhabiting a virtual world while ignoring the real one. We hear of the proliferation of on-line pornography that serves as a cheap though intoxicating substitute for genuine relationships.[16] Perhaps not surprisingly, we hear of so-called "incels," young men who are "involuntarily celibate," who, for various reasons, feel condemned to singleness without any credible possibility of a future wife and family. Of course, these incels are generally white, male, and heterosexual, so in the pantheon of the aggrieved, they don't count for much, but the despair is nonetheless real, as are the social consequences.

The despair is also traceable, in part, to a culture of immediacy whereby thought for the future is clouded by concern for the moment. Some of our most prevalent technologies foster this disposition. We have come to expect that every question can be immediately answered by Google, that every inclination can be immediately satisfied by Amazon, that communication must be instantaneous, and that friendship is always available via Facebook. We want immediate gratification, easy profit, and minimal effort. Our ubiquitous smart phones train us to be easily distracted and constantly cruising, looking for a brief informational

15. See Sommeiller and Price, "The New Gilded Age." Also, Kotkin, "America's Drift toward Feudalism," and Kotkin, *The Coming of Neo-Feudalism.*

16. See Gorby, "A Science-Based Case for Ending the Porn Epidemic," and Kristof, "The Children of Pornhub."

hookup that quickly loses its novelty and is replaced by whatever pops up next. We "surf" on-line, an apt expression connoting the fact that we skim along the surface of things, never settling long enough to find satisfaction, never imagining that satisfaction might best be realized by seeking to comprehend that which lies below the surface. Where once "settling" was seen as a good thing representing stability and focus, today "settling" is a term suggesting a lack of drive or ambition. "Keep your options open," we are told. Only losers settle. But infinitely open options preclude satisfactions that only come in the wake of commitment. The despair grows out of the dissatisfaction, but we steadfastly avoid treating the source of our anxious longings.

Such a condition is unlivable. "Someone other than myself must be to blame for the emptiness that plagues me. Surely the problem can't be me." This urge to locate a scapegoat is a persistent feature of our social moment. In times of egalitarian aspirations, one obvious scapegoat is the wealthy. It was Tocqueville who pointed out that envy is a persistent temptation in a democratic age.[17] In democratic times equality is loved even more than freedom.[18] Inequalities are seen as an indication of a fundamentally unjust system. Those who have more power, status, or material goods must be "cut down to size." They must be reduced, brought down, equalized. Envy is a gnawing vice that is constantly offended by the unavoidable fact that perfect equality is unattainable. Even as conditions become more equalized, the remaining inequalities become glaring reminders of the unfinished project of making all things equal. The frenzy of envy and the demand to eradicate all inequalities energizes a passionate and never-ending quest. When the instruments of government are brought to bear on this project, the potential for mischief is as limitless as the power of the state and the energy of the self-righteous people who make egalitarianism their life mission.

Of course, any project born of a vice must necessarily be compromised. This is not to say that all urges to equality are harmful. Seeking to pull some people down for the sake of egalitarian envy is one thing. It is entirely another thing to attempt to bring people toward greater equality by lifting up those in need or, perhaps more realistically, by helping equip the poor to succeed. For if equality is simply enforced by state power, it

17. Tocqueville, *Democracy in America*, 189.

18. Tocqueville, *Democracy in America*, 482.

remains tenuous even if material conditions are equalized. Entitlements and achievements are not simply interchangeable.

Today inequality is seen as an offense. Even inegalitarian modes of thought need to be rooted out if a truly just and equal society is to be achieved. This is why, for instance, freedom of speech is increasingly questioned as a value.[19] It is also why "hate speech" has emerged as an accusation that effectively shuts down debate, for why waste time debating "haters"? They are clearly evil and don't merit the consideration that a serious debate would require. Tolerance is merely a transitional virtue that eventually proves inadequate, for one only tolerates what one disapproves. But disapproval implies judgmentalism, which implies the belief that some positions or ways of life are superior to others. This view undermines the splendid equality for which the Socialist longs. Disapproval equals hate, and hate must be replaced by love, which is merely another way of saying that all differences are meaningless and no choice is preferable to any other—except the choice to insist that some choices are preferable to others. And therein lies the persistent grit that subconsciously worries the Woke Socialist ideologue. When love comes to mean indifference, and preferences come to mean hate, the meaning has been effectively stripped from these concepts. Only the urge to dominate remains.

The despair and anxiety felt by so many can be employed as a catalyst for a power grab of stunning breadth. When Covid fears along with climate-change worries are combined with claims of systemic injustices that include inequalities of material goods and unequal access to the levers of power, the entire system seems ripe for a replacement. The political, economic, and social structures are all implicated. The fear and insecurity so many feel can, so we are told, be remedied by a revolutionary transformation that will wean us from fossil fuels, save us from the greed of the corporations, and supplant the rapacious habits born of toxic masculinity, patriarchy, and whiteness. The term that has come to encapsulate this brave new world of social justice and wokeness is "socialism," and it stands as an indictment of the present unjust system lumped rather inelegantly under the banner of capitalism. Clearly, we are dealing with concepts that extend far beyond economics.

However, even this expansive understanding of socialism has at its core a set of economic concerns. Inequality is, perhaps, most evident

---

19. *Knight Foundation*, "Free Expression on Campus."

when it is manifest in material terms. The ownership of property has long been seen as a fundamental part of the so-called American dream. The ownership of a home, a small business, the tools of one's trade, a family farm—these have historically been seen as crucial indicators of success and the means by which economic security could be achieved. When private property comes to be increasingly concentrated in the hands of a ruling class, those who are concerned with equality will become increasingly vexed. They will see growing disparities in wealth as an indication of a system that carries injustice in its very DNA. Thus, even though the Woke Socialists extend their concerns well beyond economic themes, they see wealth disparity (and hence power disparity) as symptomatic of a sick system desperately in need of a socialist overhaul. The conditions for this socialist shift have been building for some time.

The financial collapse of 2008 was the culmination of a long, though often unseen, process that, among other things, seemed to highlight the fragile nature of property. Between January 1 and October 11, 2008, U.S. corporations lost over a third of their value. Net worth plummeted. Retirement accounts were decimated. Many Americans were forced to reorder their lives to compensate for this dramatic loss in wealth. Many more were forced to confront the hard truth that their wealth was far less secure than they had imagined. Because (or perhaps in spite) of massive government efforts to stabilize the economy, the stock market eventually recovered. Yet we were left with an obvious question: if the ownership of private property ostensibly lies at the heart of the American system—something most Americans once believed without question—and if private property can evaporate overnight, then is the American way of life as fragile and capricious as the stock market? Could it be, as our new socialists claim, that the American dream has been revealed for the charade it really is? Perhaps the events of recent years have merely served to tear down the façade of our meritocracy and reveal its rotten, plutocratic core.

The events of 2008–9 ignited a storm of responses. Groups on both the political right and left seemed to recognize that something was amiss. In the spring of 2009 the so-called Tea Party movement came to life. It was initially a rough coalition of concerned citizens who were worried that some unnamed Rubicon was about to be crossed and that the nature of the American republic was about to fundamentally change. Words like "socialism" and "communism" were employed in an attempt to describe what they feared. At root was a sense that Big Government threatened the future of freedom. Inextricably tied to these concerns was the belief that private property was under attack from those motivated by ill-conceived ideas of social justice and egalitarianism. When accusations of socialism were leveled at the Obama administration by people sympathetic with the Tea Party Movement, the concern centered on a loss of freedom as government expanded to satisfy the demands, as well as the perceived needs, of the citizenry.

On the left, the Occupy Wall Street movement was concerned with the dangerous size of Big Business and the injustices created in a world where the "one-percenters" held most of the power and the rest were merely the unwilling pawns in a game over which they have little control. While some argued that Big Government and Big Business were in collusion, the emphasis was on the scale and corruption of Business.

In 2015 Bernie Sanders, a little-known Senator from Vermont, burst onto the national scene. His Democratic Party primary challenge to Hillary Clinton was all the more remarkable given his self-professed socialism. By the time Clinton finally prevailed, Sanders had won 23 primaries and caucuses and over 40 percent of the pledged delegates. His supporters tended to be young, educated, and passionate. In fact, Sanders received more votes from those under 30 than Trump or Clinton combined.[20] He built his case around the fundamental injustice of gross inequalities of wealth and consequent power. He argued that wealth disparity in America seriously compromised our democratic system. Sanders branded himself a democratic socialist, one who sought to strengthen our democracy by employing socialist means. In short, he offered socialism as a remedy for plutocracy.

Ironically (or perhaps not), the Republican candidate in the same cycle was Donald Trump, a billionaire developer, hotelier, casino operator, and reality television star. In some ways Trump embodied the worries of Sanders: wealth equals access to power regardless of personal qualities or merit. The socialist Sanders lost in the primaries, and the capitalist Trump stunned millions when he defeated Hilary Clinton.

One might conclude that Trump's victory in 2016 represented a final repudiation of socialism. However, the election of Trump brought new energy and focus to what had previously seemed only a fringe movement, for it seemed to confirm the intuition of many that wealth provides access to power. The 2018 congressional election saw a wave of young

20. Blake, "More Young People Voted for Bernie Sanders."

candidates who without embarrassment and with little nuance referred to themselves as socialists. As the 2020 presidential campaign lurched to life, the Democratic Party seemed animated by a new gravitational force pulling both rhetoric and policies toward the socialist corner of the field that had until recent years been occupied only by radical cranks, wild-eyed graduate students, and an obscure senator from Vermont. The tide seemed to be turning, and those who championed free markets, competition, and private property were on the defensive. The landscape became even more fertile for the expansion of government into the economy with the advent of the coronavirus. The election of Joe Biden in 2020 emboldened the progressive wing of the Democratic Party and paved the way for the implementation of their bold new world. Central to this transformative project was a multi-pronged attack on private property, often justified by appeals to insecurity.

Take, for example, the moratorium on tenant evictions precipitated by the on-going Covid crisis. In March of 2020, Congress passed the Coronavirus Aid, Relief, and Economic Security Act (CARES)—who comes up with these gently reassuring acronyms? One feature of this legislation was "a 120-day eviction moratorium for properties that participated in federal assistance programs or were secured by federally backed mortgage loans." When Congress did not renew this moratorium, the Center for Disease Control (CDC) rode to the rescue by claiming that its mission to protect public health implied the power to extend and expand the moratorium. "The CDC order broadly covered all residential properties nationwide and imposed criminal penalties on violators."[21] When the law was challenged, the Supreme Court agreed that the CDC had overstepped its authority; however, Justice Kavanaugh noted that "clear and specific congressional authorization (via new legislation) would be necessary for the CDC to extend the moratorium past July 31."[22] While it is, perhaps, reassuring that the Supreme Court determined that the CDC had gone too far, it is at the same time remarkable that a "conservative" justice would suggest that an act of Congress could grant power to the CDC to continue the moratorium. In sum, the right of property owners to control their own property was rescinded in the name of public health and, by an act of Congress, could be rescinded again. The practical effect of this moratorium is the transfer of property ownership to the

21. Shatz and Ramey, "Supreme Court Strikes Down CDC Moratorium."

22. Kavanaugh, "Concurring in Alabama Association of Realtors v. Department of Health and Human Services."

government. Or to put matters more precisely, an insolent plutocracy confiscated property to placate mass insecurity at the expense of the middle class.[23] If there is not a concerted and organized pushback, it is difficult to imagine where such transfers will stop, for security threats—both real and fabricated—are ubiquitous.

Something is obviously wrong. Somehow the ideal of independence, facilitated by the ownership of productive property, has been replaced by a sense of insecurity that has translated into a steadily increasing demand for social services to restore the security for which we all long. The demand has, not surprisingly, facilitated the dramatic expansion of state power.

It is essential that we recognize an oft overlooked fact: economic centralization and political centralization feed off one another. Far from being antagonistic, they are natural allies. The history of the twentieth century shows that the massive regulatory state emerged with the explosive growth of corporate capitalism. When Republicans object that federal government intervention in the economy is destructive of liberty, they are largely right. But they fail to see that by embracing the corporatization of the economy they have aided the growth of government and, indeed, made it necessary. On the other hand, when Democrats express concern about the degrading effects of corporate capitalism, they are saying something vitally important, but they seem blind to the threat to freedom caused by an ever-expanding state.

Here we get to the root of the problem. Historically, the Left has tended to be suspicious of Big Business but trusts Big Government to rein in abuses; the Right has expressed suspicion of Big Government but shown little fear of economic centralization. However, the lines between Big Government and Big Business have become increasingly blurred. In the process, the critiques of Big Business from the Left and Big Government from the Right have become increasingly vague and unconvincing. Nevertheless, it is essential to recognize that concentrations of power in *any* form are a threat to liberty. The concentration of economic power (accompanied by concentrations of political power) implies the consolidation of private property into fewer and fewer hands and establishes the conditions that make plutocracy almost inevitable. When real private property, namely capital, becomes increasingly concentrated, the general

---

23. Broady, Edelberg, and Moss, "An Eviction Moratorium Hurts Smaller Landlords."

taste for it will eventually wane while demands for government welfare programs will increase. At that moment, freedom itself is in jeopardy.

Some, however, are coming to realize that to attack Big Government without simultaneously attacking consolidated economic power is to tilt at windmills. And, conversely, to attack Big Business and ignore the threat of Big Government is sheer foolishness. It is essential to reverse the consolidation of both political power and economic power in order to restore a vibrant culture of private property that is a necessary condition for a healthy democracy.

The thesis of this book is simple: democracy without private property is fundamentally unstable and will not survive. To put matters a bit more expansively: a proletarianized citizenry is incompatible with the republican form of government established by the U.S. Constitution. Without an effective majority of citizens who own property and whose characters have been shaped by property ownership—a vibrant middle class—the Founders' Constitution will not survive. Our current age of plutocratic socialism is a specific manifestation of a pathology the Founders feared.

No one saw this Achilles Heel of democracy better than Karl Marx. He argued that the first step in the communist revolution was to "win the battle of democracy."[24] This democratic victory required a fundamental social change: the populace needed to become proletarian, which is to say, insecure wage laborers bereft of capital. Once that occurred, the democratic process would initiate the revolution, property would be socialized, and society would be fundamentally transformed. When Tocqueville visited America in 1831, he was impressed by the fact that Americans were a propertied people. In America, he declared, there is no proletarian class.[25] This is no longer the case.

Rather than thinking about private property from the perspective of economics, which suggests concepts such as efficiency, GDP, and growth, I want to consider property from the perspective of politics, which suggests concepts such as power, citizenship, virtue, equality, and freedom. It is from this perspective that I will argue that broadly disseminated private property is an indispensable ingredient for a society of free citizens.

From this perspective, the rancorous conflict between Democrats and Republicans takes on new meaning. Many Republicans insist that our current situation is merely the result of market forces combined with

24. Marx, *The Marx-Engels Reader*, 490.
25. Tocqueville, *Democracy in America*, 228.

a meritocracy wherein rewards are doled out based on nothing but hard work and talent. They insist that massive corporate power and growing income inequality are the natural outcomes produced by the market's invisible (but always just) hand. It is, in this light, no surprise that many Democrats smell a rat. If this is capitalism, it clearly needs replacing. Woke Socialism has emerged to provide an alternative to the injustices seemingly latent in American society. But what if both sides are wrong? What if the thing many on the right identify as capitalism is a corrupt and unstable facsimile that has retained some of the outward features of a market system but has steadily eroded middle-class property, which is its essence? What if socialism holds out the promise of justice and equality only to destroy freedom in the end? And perhaps most striking: what if the two reigning alternatives actually serve to enable and strengthen each other? What if the corporatization of the economy produces insecure, proletarianized citizens who quite understandably demand the social and economic security that only a strong state can provide? In short, what if the ascending plutocracy is a natural outgrowth of concentrations of wealth, on the one hand, combined with the resulting insecure, property-less citizenry on the other? From this perspective, it appears that property arrangements that make plutocracy more or less inevitable are the same that make socialist policies attractive.

Ultimately, the fate of the American constitutional order and, more broadly, of freedom itself depends on the fate of private property. As citizens increasingly demand services rendered by the omni-benevolent hand of the state working in concert with corporate power, the longing for private property will fade; after all, the state promises to care for every need, including our daily bread. The fear and uncertainty of a world-wide pandemic, racial unrest, and a climate apocalypse serve only to acceler-ate the process. When the longing for private property is eclipsed by the demand for social services and social security, the demise of freedom is nigh. The welfare state will continue to expand along the socialist continuum, for the more dependents brought under its care, the more constituents it will have to validate its existence at the ballot box.

There is another way. It is a harder road but it is rooted in the best of American ideals. It is a way that recognizes that with freedom comes the responsibility to act in ways becoming of free men and women. It is a way that grasps that private property is the lynchpin of a free society. It is a way that knows the promises of security and plenty made by the state cost more than free people are willing to pay.

In the end, the viability of our freedom depends on the degree to which we cherish and possess private property. For when we have lost the taste for calling something our own and caring for it with responsibility born of affection, we will find that the freedom we claim as our right is merely an empty husk, incapable of sustaining either us or the American republic.

Chapter One

Private Property

An Enduring Concept

Big government and big business have developed together in Western society, and each has depended on the other.

—ROBERT NISBET

WE ALL KNOW SOMETHING about private property. When a toddler grabs his favorite toy and declares "mine!" he is expressing a universal human impulse. When Jones polishes the new car in his driveway and gazes at it with satisfaction, he is keenly aware that it is *his*. It is not community property that others can use whenever they please. Simply defined, *private property* is that to which I have an exclusive right. It *belongs* to me and not to anyone else. A house, perhaps, visually demonstrates this idea better than anything else, for a house has walls behind which we conduct our private lives. If a person attempts to enter our home without permission, we recognize immediately that something important is being violated. Some states even have so-called "Castle Doctrines" that allow for the use of deadly force to prevent forcible entry into one's home.

While philosophers and politicians have long debated the details of private property, in simple terms it's not hard to see how all of us require some property in order to live. An apple growing on a tree in the wild might not belong to anyone, but when I pick the apple, its status changes. We would intuitively condemn the person who walked up to me after I plucked the apple and grabbed it out of my hand. When I take a bite of the apple, chew it, and swallow it, the "mineness" becomes indisputable as the apple is incorporated into my body. Thus, in the very process of eating we make some things our own. At some point, we acquire exclusive right to the food we eat.

Private property, of course, extends far beyond what we eat. We think of our personal effects in terms of property. "This is my toothbrush" implies "and no one else is free to use it." In making such a claim we draw an invisible but real circle around the item. We fence it off from the rest of humanity and expect that barrier to be respected. When that barrier is violated, we object: "Hey, that's *mine!*" Parents invariably hear variations of the plaintive "Mom! Jimmy took my crayon!"

Historically, land represents the quintessential form of private property, for out of the land come the various means by which life is sustained. Land produces food, both for humans and livestock. It provides trees for building material and firewood. Surplus foodstuffs and timber can be sold or traded for items not directly produced by the land. A fence, a hedge, a stone wall, or simple boundary markers serve to indicate the extent of our property and distinguish it from property belonging to someone else.

Some have argued that property extends beyond physical items to include ideas and concepts. Thus, copyright laws protect words and ideas assembled in a particular way. James Madison argued that people have property in their rights.[1] That is, all people *possess* certain "unalienable" rights and these rights belong to a person just as surely as the plot of land inherited from a father.

Some have suggested that people hold property rights over their own bodies. To be sure, my left arm belongs to me in an obvious way: no one has a right to use it without my permission. No one can rightly take it from me or destroy it apart from my consent (and, short of gangrene, it's hard to imagine why I would consent). At the same time, the idea of bodily ownership does raise questions. Some have argued that we belong to God and thus we are not absolutely free to use our bodies as we like: we hold them in trust as stewards. Yet even apart from this theological position, it does seem that ownership of our own bodies is somewhat different from, say, ownership of a ballpoint pen. For one thing, I care more about my body than I do about any pen. But more than that, it's not entirely clear that I simply *have* a body so much as I *am* a body and

---

1. Madison, *The Writings of James Madison*, 101–3.

a soul. René Descartes suggested that an immaterial mind or soul drives the body like a captain pilots a ship, but our lived experience suggests that the relationship between mind (or soul) and body is much closer. In fact, a sick body can make the soul miserable and a miserable soul can sicken the body. A human, then, appears to be an amalgam, a unity of body and soul. Bodies may be something to which we have exclusive right, but reducing them merely to the status of private property doesn't do justice to them—if, in fact, my body is an essential part of what I *am* rather than simply something I *have*.

Such debates, if nothing else, indicate that the idea of private property is more complicated than might first appear. However, setting aside for now the rather complex metaphysical question of bodily ownership, we can summarize the discussion quite simply: our daily lives are full of instances where we act as if we possess private property. To live otherwise would seem, at least on the face of things, to be impossible. Yet to grasp the full meaning of private property, as well as the ways it is under threat today, we do well to examine how the concept has developed through history. The following is a cursory overview, but it will indicate some of the ways people have thought about property and thereby provide us with the necessary context to consider modern attacks on private property.

Human affairs naturally give rise to notions of property. Antiquity provides us with both illustrations and justifications for property ownership. The simple act of exchanging gifts requires ownership, for a gift is only possible if real ownership passes from one person to another. In the *Iliad*, for instance, Glaucos (a Trojan) and Diomedes (a Greek) come face to face on the field of battle. Before setting upon each other, they take a moment to boast of their lineage. In the process they discover that their grandfathers were friends. So instead of fighting to the death they exchange gifts.[2] Such gift-giving rests on the assumption—clearly present at the dawn of western civilization—that ownership can rightly be transferred because property can rightfully be owned.

Related to gift-giving is the virtue of generosity. Aristotle, whose moral philosophy centers on the excellences of character he calls virtues, argues that an excellent man is a generous man, willing to give of his own possessions. Additionally, he describes a virtue that some translators call "magnificence," denoting one who practices giving on a large scale.

2. *Iliad*, Book VI, lines 146–295.

Such a man gives to support public projects and sponsor public festivals. In short, when generosity entails the giving of material goods, private property is a necessary antecedent.[3]

Aristotle held that the acquisition of property was a vital function of household management. Early in the development of human societies, exchange of surplus production naturally emerged as a means to supplement the goods of a household. Money was developed to provide a convenient means of exchange. Households exist to provide for everyday needs, and property is necessary for the existence of households. Thus, for Aristotle, property is a natural component of human society.[4]

According to the Bible, God created the first humans, Adam and Eve, in His own image and placed them in a garden. God gives them "dominion" over all the other living creatures. This dominion suggests a prerogative to rule the Creation as God's regents. The man and woman are given the responsibility to steward that which ultimately belongs to God. Furthermore, "God said, Behold, I have given you every herb bearing seed, which is upon the face of all the earth, and every tree, in the which is the fruit of a tree yielding seed; to you it shall be for meat." In the same way God declares that "I have given every green herb" to the beasts for their food.[5] While property ownership may not be explicitly the focus, the concept plays an essential role. God presumably owns His Creation, and one feature of ownership is dominion. When God creates humans in His own image and grants them dominion over the Creation, He is granting them, as a gift, the right to rule. This right implies a sort of ownership over the Creation. This ownership is made explicit when God "gives" the man and woman all edible plants for their sustenance. The fact that God also gives the animals that which is properly food for them suggests that the property owned by humans is not absolute or exclusive but must be understood within the context of a created order.

In the Biblical story of Cain and Abel (the first two sons of Adam and Eve), property plays a central role. The brothers bring to God an offering of their property: Cain brings the fruit of the soil, and Abel brings a lamb. God is pleased with Abel but not Cain, and in a fit of jealous rage Cain murders Abel. While the reason God favors lamb over cabbage is not clear, the assumption underlying the story is that private property is

---

3. Aristotle, *Nicomachean Ethics*, Book IV, ch. 1–2.

4. Aristotle, *Politics*, Book I, ch. 8–9.

5. Genesis 1: 26, 29, 30. Italics added.

legitimate, and God has a proper claim to at least a share.[6] Thus, the first inter-human conflict—resulting in violence and bloodshed—turns on a dispute over the appropriate use of property.

This understanding of private property is interwoven into the context of the biblical world. Abram separated his flocks from those of Lot and went to the hills, while Lot took his possessions and settled on the plains near Sodom.[7] Jacob made an agreement with his father-in-law, Laban, that he would manage his herds if all the streaked or spotted animals would be added to Jacob's possessions. Laban agreed, lots of streaky animals were born, and Jacob's private property increased dramatically.[8] In the Mosaic Law, private property is again simply assumed. "Thou shalt not steal" presumes the existence of property.[9] God gives detailed laws dictating specific punishments for theft and the amount of restitution required for damaging the property of another.[10] These laws indicate that private property was the norm.

The issue of property is, however, not simply a one-way street. The Mosaic Law explicitly limits the use of property. For instance, harvesters are commanded not to reap to the very edge of their fields, and owners of vineyards are commanded not to go over the vineyards a second time or pick up the fruit that has fallen to the ground. These are to be left behind for the poor and the alien. In short, ownership of property includes responsibility to the community, which entails limits on the use of one's own property.[11]

The Hebrew prophets spend a surprising amount of time berating those who mistreat the poor, those who ignore widows and orphans and other unfortunates bereft of property. Such a teaching, again, assumes that individuals who possess property should help those in need. Generosity is praised while hoarding is condemned.[12]

One of the most explicit and memorable images of the social and political effects of private property is found in the prophet Micah. As the prophet envisions a world of peace and security, he looks forward to

6. Genesis 4.

7. Genesis 13.

8. Genesis 30.

9. Exodus 20:15.

10. Exodus 22.

11. Leviticus 19:9–10.

12. See, for instance, Micah and Amos.

a time when people "shall beat their swords into plowshares, and their spears into pruninghooks: nation shall not lift up a sword against nation, neither shall they learn war any more." Coming directly on the heels of this vision of peace is a concrete expression of the social and economic conditions for individual security: "They shall sit every man under his vine and under his fig tree; and none shall make them afraid."[13] When each man is able to sit at peace under his own vine—the source of wine— and under his own fig tree—a source of food—then the conditions exist for a truly secure and peaceful society. Ownership of the means of production is tied to the peace and security of citizens. This passage, incidentally, was frequently quoted by Americans in the period leading up to the American War for Independence. They understood that this compact description of peace and property contained the key idea for which they were willing to sacrifice and die.

Of course, not all ancient thinkers enthusiastically embraced private property. Perhaps the most famous example is Plato, the teacher of Aristotle. In his book-length dialogue, *The Republic*, Plato argues that private property is disruptive of social unity. Plato is attempting to imagine a perfect society, one in which each person performs the function that nature has equipped him to perform. The leaders of this society, as well as those tasked with protecting it from foreign threats, must remain steadfast in their commitments. They must not be distracted by wealth, and they must work exclusively for the benefit of the community. Private property, according to Plato, is the primary source of disunity, for it induces citizens to say "this is mine" and in the process to set themselves apart from other citizens.[14] It is this temptation to exclusivity that leads Plato to suggest that even marriage is a problem, that all men and all women should belong to each other, and children should be regarded as the children of all.

Scholars have spilt much ink (though not much blood) attempting to grasp what Plato is doing in this utopian tract. Some claim that Plato has no intention that such a utopia should ever be attempted. This line of argument finds some support when we examine certain passages in Plato's work of practical politics, *The Laws*. At times the utopianism of the *Republic* is evident. However, at other times Plato takes a much more conventional approach to private property, as well as to marriage and

13. Micah 4:3, 4.

14. Plato, *Republic*, 462b–c.

family life. Plato argues that gross disparity of private property creates instability. Yet he does not advocate simple equality. He recognizes that differences in ability, effort, and birth (not to mention luck) will lead to differences in property holdings. Nevertheless, the health of a society will tend to decline when some citizens are without property while others amass great wealth.[15] As we will see, the question of inequality is never far removed from the discussion of private property.

In the Sermon on the Mount, Christ extols his hearers to give in secret and not with great fanfare. Giving, in other words, should come from the heart and be motivated by love rather than desire for fame or reputation.[16] St. Paul warns his fellow Christians about the love of money, but he also affirms that it is good to be content with simple possessions.[17] St. James teaches that true religion includes looking after widows and orphans.[18] An important way this is accomplished is through opening one's home to the homeless and by giving food and clothing to the hungry and naked. Again, private property is simply assumed, but at the same time ownership of property includes responsibilities to the poor and destitute.

The New Testament church described in the book of Acts presents a challenge to the idea of private property. The new believers sold all their possessions and gave to anyone in need. They held possessions in common. They spent their days meeting in the temple courts; they lived and prayed together and enjoyed common meals.[19] However, these arrangements appear to have been short-lived. These early Christians (they weren't even called Christians at this point) believed that Jesus would return at any time. They were looking for the coming of a new kingdom, and they expected it to appear immediately. It didn't take long for these new converts to realize that perhaps what Christ meant by "soon" was not what they imagined. Private property, along with the social responsibilities that come with property ownership, was clearly the norm prior to the time of Christ and soon after his passion. The teachings of the early church, like those of the Mosaic Law, consistently include exhortations to help the poor and to practice generosity and hospitality, both of which assume ownership.

15. Plato, *Laws*, 744–5.

16. Matthew 6:1–4.

17. I Timothy 6: 6–10.

18. James 1: 27.

19. Acts 2: 42–47.

Some monastic orders, of course, limit or exclude private property among their members. Indeed, various communities throughout the centuries (usually religious in nature) have held property in common. The results have been mixed. Some have thrived while others have fallen apart and disbanded. Importantly, these communities have been voluntary. There is a world of difference between common property among members of a voluntary society and the abolition of private property at the insistence of the state.

The medieval Christian thinker St. Thomas Aquinas did not hesitate to affirm the goodness of private property. He understood that individuals take better care of things they own. Unowned property or property held in common, he noted, tends to suffer neglect, abuse, and exploitation. Aquinas further argued that human affairs tend to be conducted in a more orderly and peaceful fashion when individuals manage and dispose of external goods that belong to them. Aquinas based his argument for the goodness of private property on the practical results that are likely to accrue in a society where property is recognized and respected.[20]

In America the idea of private property runs like a crimson thread through the annals of our history. The earliest settlers to our shores were motivated by a longing for freedom, and they understood that political freedom was tied inextricably to economic freedom. To claim the former without the latter was to grasp at a vapor, an imagined good but not a tangible reality. The seemingly endless land of the North American continent suggested a new world teeming with possibilities lying dormant until roused by energetic and creative hands.

The American War of Independence was fought because of the perceived injustice of a system that required the colonists to submit to the dictates of the British Parliament while having no voice in that body. The rallying cry "no taxation without representation" was not a new or novel concept. The principle can be traced back into English common law and was simply a reiteration of the idea that taxes may not be levied without the consent of the governed. In other words, the people, through their representatives, have the final say in matters relating to their property.

This principle lay at the core of John Locke's political theory. Locke was an English philosopher whose work was widely read in the years leading up to the American Revolution. In the wake of the Glorious Revolution in England Locke published his *Second Treatise on Civil Government*

---

20. Aquinas, *Summa Theologica*, II-II, Question 66, Articles 1–2.

in which he develops an account of government arising from what he termed a "state of nature." In this hypothetical original state all of the earth was held in common. All people were free and equal, and as long as they lived according to the laws of nature, they could get along without government. Individuals could appropriate property from the commons by mixing their labor with it. Thus, if I clear a field, sow seeds, and water and cultivate the soil, the field, as well as the harvest, belongs to me. Locke stipulates that this process of appropriation exists only to the extent that I leave "enough and as good" in the commons so that others have the same opportunity to acquire property that I did. Furthermore, if for instance I gather fruit from the commons, the law of nature forbids that I gather more than I can use before it spoils. Thus, there are natural limits to the amount of property I can legitimately acquire. But, as Locke points out, with the invention of money, I can exchange the property that is prone to spoil for that which is not susceptible to decay. Thus, the invention of money eliminates the limitation on acquisition originally imposed by the law of nature. Locke's account of property arguably leads to an unlimited acquisition of property and in the process legitimates the extreme in-equalities that many today find so problematic.

Locke argued that all people have the right to life, liberty, and prop-erty. These rights were, according to Locke, not easily separated. After all, an attack on my private property is surely an attack on my liberty, for private property provides one means by which I exercise my liberty. Furthermore, if someone is willing to attack my liberty, how can I be cer-tain that my life will not be in jeopardy as well? He who seeks to remove my liberty is probably not concerned with my life, unless he wants to enslave me and thereby make me his property. Locke has an expansive view of property and, in fact, lumps various basic rights under that head. "Government," he writes, "has no other end but the preservation of prop-erty." This includes people's "lives, liberties, and estates, which I call by the general name, property."[21]

The language of Locke finds its way into the Declaration of Inde-pendence with a small modification. Thomas Jefferson wrote that all men are endowed by God with certain rights, and among these are the rights to "Life, Liberty, and the Pursuit of Happiness." On one hand, the replacement of "property" with "the pursuit of happiness" might seem a serious oversight, for if property is essential to liberty, to omit property is

21. John Locke, *Second Treatise*, §123.

to curtail liberty itself. Yet if the two are as intimately conjoined as Locke suggests, then the phrase "pursuit of happiness" must be understood to include all those things pertaining to our happiness. Liberty rooted in private property is one of those things. This view is further strengthened by the rest of the Declaration, where several of the particular indictments against King George center on unjust confiscation of property through taxation and other means. Indeed, without freedom the pursuit of happiness is impossible, and without property the pursuit of happiness is severely constricted.

These notions make it clear why the issue of slavery produced such tension in the United States. To claim property in another person is simultaneously to claim that the exercise of my freedom can encompass another person. The slave, meanwhile, is denied the very human aspiration to be free and to own property for himself (and in himself). A nation championing the idea of freedom could not forever tolerate the legal reduction of an entire class of people to the status of private property.

Less than a century after Locke wrote, and in the same year the colonies in America declared their independence from Britain, Adam Smith published *An Inquiry into the Nature and Causes of the Wealth of Nations* (often shortened to *The Wealth of Nations*). Like the state-of-nature theorists who preceded him, Smith attempted to provide an account of advanced societies by first describing the primitive societies out of which they emerged.

Smith famously begins his book with these lines: "The greatest improvement in the productive powers of labour, and the greater part of the skill, dexterity, and judgment with which it is any where directed, or applied, seem to have been the effects of the division of labour."[22] The manufacture of pins, for example, is made far more efficient if the division of labor is employed. Consider, for instance, if one person was tasked with making a pin from scratch. He would begin by mining and refining the ore. He would then need to form the iron into thin lengths from which he would fashion a pin. The entire task would be arduous. Even the most industrious person would be hard pressed to average a few pins a day.

The division of labor is a principle that emerged out of the exclusively human tendency "to truck, barter, and exchange one thing for another."[23] Trade is motivated by self-interest. Both parties in a typical

---

22. Smith, *Wealth of Nations*, vol. I, 13.
23. Smith, *Wealth of Nations*, vol. I, 25.

exchange seek to improve themselves, and ideally both sides are pleased with the outcome. The free exchange of goods presupposes the existence of clearly delineated property rights, for if the title to a potential object of exchange is uncertain, the legitimacy of the exchange is thrown into question. Although in a free market inequalities are inevitable, Smith is convinced that the social good produced by free markets will benefit all, from the meanest laborer to the wealthiest industrialist.

The industrial revolution introduced steam power and factories. Unskilled labor could now perform the majority of the work. The long-acquired skill of the artisan was replaced by those who performed a simple and mindless task for twelve hours or more a day. Unskilled labor, of course, comes cheaper than skilled labor, and with a surplus of labor and a dearth of laws protecting laborers from abuse, conditions in some industries were deplorable. Don't like the wages? Too bad. There are plenty of other unskilled workers in line for your job. Injured on the job? Tough luck. The fiction of Dickens is rife with gritty characters living on the hard side of this economic equation.

It was during this time that Marx wrote his scathing rebuke of capitalism in general and private property in particular. He was disgusted with the squalid conditions of the laboring class. He sought to provide an account of history and institutions that made sense of the present situation and imagined a future state where the capitalist class would be overthrown, workers emancipated, and private property abolished. Marx's sweeping vision is every bit as utopian as that of Plato's *Republic*.

Marx argued that when a society is divided into two economic classes—the bourgeoisie who own capital and the proletariat who do not—abuse is inevitable. Because of the division of labor, the wage laborer is alienated from his efforts. He may never even see the final product into which he has poured his time and energy. The capitalist will pay barely subsistence wages, only enough to keep the miserable wretches who work for him alive. This situation represents, according to Marx, a kind of slavery. The wage-slave pours his life into a product that is forever separated from him. He will never feel the satisfaction of handling it or signing his name to it, much less be able to use it or profit from its sale.

According to Marx, the rise of the machine made this alienated existence more possible and more widespread: "owing to the extensive use of machinery and to division of labor, the work of the proletarians has lost all individual character, and consequently, all charm for the workman. He becomes an appendage of the machine, and it is only the most simple, most monotonous, and most easily acquired knack, that is required of him."[24] The "little workshop" is replaced by the great factory, and workers become indistinguishable from one another. Differences of age and sex disappear, for the nature of the work requires no such distinctions.

Marx's solution is to abolish, via revolution, the entire economic system that makes such abuses and miseries possible. He would emancipate workers by emancipating society from private property. The proletarians, he writes, "have nothing of their own to secure and to fortify."[25] They have nothing to tie them to the current system, no incentive to improve their condition in the context of the capitalist structure. They will, according to Marx, have every incentive to destroy the system that has ground them down so ruthlessly. The revolution predicted by Marx is a revolution of the working class against their capitalist overlords. In the wake of this revolutionary upheaval, a new social existence will emerge in which private property (specifically private capital) will disappear, in which all are free to live according to their own desires and abilities, and in which each individual is equal to all others. The state will wither away.

The events of the twentieth century, however, provide ample evidence to suggest that Marx's solution is simply incompatible with reality. No communist state ever withered away (although some fell to ruin from internal decay and external pressure). No communist revolution ever got beyond the revolutionary phase; none ever realized the radical equality, happiness, and freedom that Marx predicted. In fact, all three ideals suffered major blows under communist rule. Instead, the various communist revolutions tended to produce ruthless plutocrats who held tenaciously to their power even at the expense of the people in whose name they ostensibly ruled.

Marx seems to have missed two important facts. First, the deplorable conditions were, in much of the industrial world, significantly remedied by the institution and enforcement of labor laws. No revolution was needed to bring about safer working conditions and shorter work weeks. Furthermore, in many sectors wages have not remained at subsistence levels. Through competition the market itself gradually produced an increase in wages so that it becomes sheer hyperbole to equate wage-laborers with wage-slaves. Second, while Marx championed the abolition of private property and with it the economic system based on the private

24. Marx, *The Marx-Engels Reader*, 479.
25. Marx, *The Marx-Engels Reader*, 482.

ownership of capital, given what we know of human nature, there are compelling reasons to suggest that a reinvigoration of private property would in fact better address his concerns.

Socialism was slow to take hold in the United States. The nation expanded westward because the possibility of land ownership—and with it the opportunity to improve one's conditions—pulled hard on the imaginations of those who found themselves impoverished, or at least dissatisfied, in the east. The purchase of the Louisiana Territory more than doubled the land belonging to the young nation. The Homestead Act of 1862 provided 160 acres free of charge to anyone who would improve it. Land was, for many, the foundational element in their pursuit of happiness, for it represented independence. Family farms, and small towns to support them, sprang up across the heartland.

Well into the twentieth century family farms continued to be a mainstay of the American economy and culture. But Jefferson, who famously extolled the virtues of the yeoman farmer, would have been disturbed by the general trend; times were changing, and the agrarian economy was gradually replaced.

With the steady march of industrialization, two world wars, and a great depression that brought to life the New Deal, changes accelerated. Mechanization and chemical fertilizers meant fewer workers could produce more food than ever before. Besides, the cities beckoned, and with improved transportation along with television and film depicting the glamourous possibilities of the city, the flow of people shifted. Where in the nineteenth century the population was moving westward and filling up the continent, by the mid-twentieth century, people—especially the young—were heading to the cities. As the twentieth century wore on, farms were consolidated, equipment got larger, and many rural communities began to atrophy and die.

But this movement away from the land did not represent an abandonment of the idea of private property. Instead, where land was the quintessential emblem of property in early America, property in the form of abstract wealth became the new norm. The possibility of acquiring diverse goods expanded as disposable income increased and small-scale farming was replaced by manufacturing and commerce. The ownership of private property seemed to expand significantly even as it took on a radically different appearance.

The shift away from the land was accompanied during the twentieth century by a steady increase in the size and scope of government.

The New Deal ushered in a vast number of programs intended to render aid to those suffering the ravages of the Depression. Three decades later, Lyndon Johnson's Great Society sought to erase the blight of poverty by expanding government programs. The Obama administration, and later the Biden administration, seemed intent on pushing the aspirations of the New Deal in even more ambitious and costly directions. All Americans, we are often told, are endowed with the right to enjoy greater wealth, comfort, and prosperity than previous generations, and Americans seem determined to demonstrate the veracity of this iron-clad law. The public spending spree echoes a private spending spree that has decimated personal savings and reduced millions of Americans to living paycheck-to-paycheck, even as they max out credit cards to purchase the newest gizmo from Apple.

Thus, the socialist dream reappeared in the form of a steadily expanding welfare state and persistent insecurity that seemed only to grow more pronounced. Like the invisible coronavirus, systemic racism is seemingly everywhere, and its presence is ineradicable. So, too, the looming climate crisis seems beyond our abilities to check, so we naturally look to the government as the only possible means of salvation. Justice, security, and equality require, we are told, the curtailment or elimination of property ownership if we are to have any hope of eliminating the disorders that plague us: inequality, economic insecurity, and even unhappiness. This dream is often accompanied by the idea that work can be eliminated or at least made optional. Today some are calling for a universal basic income regardless of employment status or willingness to work.[26] In 2020 the World Economic Forum launched an ad campaign that included eight predictions for 2030. The first: "You'll own nothing. And you'll be happy."[27] The examples abound, but the common thread joining these various policy proposals is a severing of humans from the tangible world of work and from a world where responsibility and care is fundamentally joined to property ownership. In place of this all too human arrangement we have a dream world where work is optional and ownership is replaced by a sharing and renting economy in which no one is bereft of property because property is unowned and undesired. Equality will finally be achieved, justice will be realized, and all will be happy.

---

26. See for instance, Collins, "Covid-19 and Universal Basic Income," and Kopf, "What's a universal basic income doing in Ocasio-Cortez's "Green New Deal"?

27. World Economic Forum, "You'll Own Nothing and You'll be Happy."

As we will see, the Woke Socialists put equality at the center of their rhetoric and policy goals. And although they speak of freedom, the freedom of pornographic expression, gender preference, or sexual identity is not the same as the freedom espoused by those who established our constitutional republic. A hearty political freedom characterized by independent and virtuous citizens is a far cry from the freedom claimed by lonely citizens demanding faster internet, more government services, and the satiation of an endless parade of desires.

Here's a question that we will very much want to keep in mind: Could the restoration of private property provide a launching point both for a reinvigorated conception of equality that does not threaten freedom and a vibrant conception of freedom that does not debase itself?

Chapter Two

Property From Jamestown to Philadelphia

Will a man throw afloat his property & confide it to a government a thousand miles *distant?*

—PIERCE BUTLER—CONSTITUTIONAL CONVENTION

THE IDEA OF PRIVATE property is inseparable from the story of America's history. In 1607 the first colony of English settlers landed at a place they named for their king, James I. This was an intrepid band of adventurers. They had heard rumors of riches in the new world, and they came to cash in. Most planned to return to England as wealthy men. No women were part of this initial foray. This was not, at least at first, an enterprise for families. The first woman arrived in the summer of 1608. A year later about twenty women arrived with their husbands.

For these adventurers the winter of 1609–10 came to be known as The Starving Time. Fierce hunger gripped the settlement, and hostile Indians threatened those who ventured out for food. Eventually they resorted to eating cats, dogs, horses, and rats. Some grave robbers allegedly sought nourishment in the flesh of fellow colonists lately expired. By the end of that desperate winter, the survivors decided to abandon the settlement. Just as they were preparing to set off, vessels arrived filled with supplies and new settlers. The beleaguered colonists were compelled by the new governor to remain in Virginia.

The general disorder of the Jamestown colony prompted the governor to declare martial law. The "Virginia Articles, Law, and Orders" instituted a draconian system of rules along with extreme punishment for lawbreakers. Some of these laws give us an idea of the various ways the colony had broken down. For example, religious belief is emphasized. Church attendance was mandatory. Blasphemy was punishable by death. "Traitorous words against his Majesties Person" received the same punishment. Sodomy and adultery were punishable by death. Fornication was punished by whipping for the first and second offense. The third instance: death. Embezzlement and price-fixing were severely punished. The squalor of the settlement must have been appalling. No "Launderer or Launderesse" shall "wash any uncleane Linnen, drive bucks [bleach clothes], or throw out the water or sudes of fowle cloathes, in the open streete, within the Pallizadoes [Pallisades], or within forty foote of thee same, nor rench [rinse], and make cleane, any kettle, pot or pan, or such like vessel within twenty foote of the olde well, or a new pump." And though it might seem to go without saying, all persons were forbidden to "doe the necessities of nature" within a quarter mile of the palisade, "since by these unmanly, slothful, and loathsome immodesties, the whole Forte may be choked, and poisoned with ill aires." Indeed.

As far as private property was concerned, robbing a garden was punishable by death. In such lean times, to steal food was not far from depriving a person of his life. Yet the notion of private property was complicated. Upon pain of death, "no man shall dare to kill, or destroy any Bull, Cow, Calfe, Mare, Horse, Colt, Goate, Swine, Cocke, Henne, Chicken, Dogge, Turkie, or any tame Cattel, or Poultry, of what condition soever; whether his owne, or appertaining to another man, without leave from the Generall." Accessories to such crimes would suffer "burning of the Hand, and losse of his eares, and unto the concealer of the same four and twenty houres of whipping, with addition of further punishment, as shall be thought fitte by the censure, and verdict of a Martiall Court."[1] These laws, were, of course, temporary remedies to real problems. The colony had to be stabilized, regular habits had to be established, and a sense of personal responsibility had to accompany ownership of property. Ownership was seen as a two-way street that included both rights and duties. Shirking the latter led to forfeiting the former.

---

1. Frohnen, ed. *The American Republic: Primary Sources*, 4–10.

Thirteen years after Jamestown was settled, a tiny band of religious dissidents set out to establish a colony "in the Northern parts of Virginia." They landed off the coast of what is today Massachusetts. These Pilgrims had embarked on their ship, *The Mayflower*, seeking religious freedom in the new world. As they expressed the matter in their Mayflower Compact, signed just prior to disembarking onto a new continent: "We whose Names are undersigned, the Loyal Subjects of our dread Sovereign Lord King James . . . Having undertaken for the glory of God, and the advancement of the Christian Faith, and the Honour of our King and Country . . . Do by these Presents, solemnly and mutually, in the presence of God and one another, Covenant and Combine our selves together into a Civil Body Politick, for our better ordering and preservation, and the furthering of the ends aforesaid." Furthermore, they committed themselves to framing "just and equal Laws" that "shall be thought most meet and convenient for the general good of the Colony; unto which we promise all due submission and obedience."[2]

The gravity of this document is obvious. The colonists were, after all, embarking on a bold venture with limited resources and no shelter. This being November, a long New England winter was just setting in. These were serious people committed to the idea that freedom to worship God in their own way was more important than any comforts they might have enjoyed in England.

This small band of religious dissenters was surely awed by the sheer quantity of land now available to them. In Europe, land was a scarce commodity, each parcel having been claimed and tamed by nobles, king, or small holder. The Pilgrims found themselves on the edge of an unexplored continent. The curious wanderer, when he summitted the highest point around, saw only dark hills and endless forests stretching away to the west. Untold acres were available to anyone willing and able to tame them.

Unlike the original settlers at Jamestown, these colonists intended to stay. They had been outcasts and misfits in England and then Holland and were intent on making a new life in the new world. They were, as the novelist Wallace Stegner put it centuries later, "stickers."[3] Stickers, in Stegner's typology, intend to remain where they've settled. On the other hand, "boomers" are continually looking ahead for the next opportunity,

---

2. Frohnen, ed. *The American Republic: Primary Sources*, 11.

3. Stegner, *Where the Bluebird Sings to the Lemonade Springs*, xi–xxviii.

the next step, and the next move. At least initially, Jamestown was populated by boomers. The Plymouth settlers were stickers from the start.

The Pilgrims originally attempted to hold all property in common, but this novelty was quickly abandoned. The Plymouth colonists settled into subsistence farming on small private holdings. Representative forms of government developed. Until 1664 citizenship was restricted to church members. Dissenters were banished (Roger Williams, for instance, left and founded Rhode Island). In 1632, freemen gained the right to directly elect the governor, and in 1668 ownership of property (specifically land) was added as a qualification to vote. Thus, the connection between property ownership and self-government was formally established. Owners of land were considered stable citizens who would vote with the long-term good of the community in mind. Furthermore, property holders could not, according to English Common Law, be taxed without their consent. For Englishmen this was a long-established and well-understood principle with origins that extended far back into the mists of English history.

June 15, 1215 is a red-letter date in the history of America. On that auspicious day when the Magna Carta was signed, the new world had yet to be discovered. Nevertheless, principles laid down in that document and reiterated in subsequent declarations provided a foundation for limiting the power of the sovereign. These principles formed the English view of just government and were eventually transmitted across the Atlantic and into the wilderness of North America.

In 1215 John was king of England. This was the same John who, according to legend, chased Robin Hood around Sherwood Forest. When John's brother Richard I (the Lion Hearted) died, John assumed the throne. John wasn't especially wise or tactful. Like most executives, he sought to expand his power. Of course, the barons pushed back, for the expansion of the king's power meant a reduction of theirs. John flaunted long-standing practices, many of which involved raising money. When matters came to a head, the king's troops were defeated by the barons, who then sent word to the king demanding that he meet them at the field of Runnemede. John didn't want to sign the document they offered him. The very act of signing such a thing indicated his relative weakness. Most importantly, it signified that the king himself was under the law and not superior to it.

The Magna Carta does not claim to invent anything new. Rather, it reiterates the customary rights and privileges claimed by the barons, the clergy, and the people for generations. These included the right of the church (and not the king) to elect bishops, the right to a trial by jury, limits on excessive fines, and the guarantee of equal justice before the law.

There are also provisions relating directly to private property. Paragraph 28 is titled "Compensation for the taking of private property." Here it is forbidden for any "constable or bailiff" to take "corn or other chattels of any man" without fair compensation. Paragraph 30 is titled "No taking of horses or carts without consent." Paragraph 31 forbids the taking of timber without consent of the owner. Taxation (as ever) is a central concern, for a right to unlimited taxation represents an implied right to unlimited power. Thus, the barons insisted that the king concede that taxes shall only be assessed with the consent of the general council. In other words, the king could not assess taxes without the consent of the barons—who, of course, were the ones being taxed. The principle of no taxation without consent embedded itself deeply into the English mind and was a central principle in the American Revolution.[4]

In 1625, a mere five years after the Pilgrims landed at Plymouth, Charles I succeeded James I as king of England. By this time the English Parliament had emerged as a formal body. The story of English history is, for some centuries, one of competition between king and parliament. As is always the case with power, both sides sought supremacy. The fortunes of both waxed and waned by turns. Charles I was ambitious and sought to assert himself and the royal prerogative. He waged a series of unpopular foreign wars, and to pay expenses he forced his wealthy subjects to chip in. Troops were quartered in private homes, and those who opposed the king's policies were imprisoned. In 1628 Parliament asserted itself by presenting the king with the Petition of Right. In this document Parliament reiterated the rights that had long been claimed (if not always enjoyed) by Englishmen, the same basic rights expressed in the Magna Carta. Parliament declared that no one should be forced to give or loan money to the crown and that no tax could be assessed except "by common consent in Parliament."[5]

Consent of Parliament represented the consent of the property holders in the kingdom. When a century and a half later the Americans asserted "no taxation without representation" they were in fact hearkening back to the principle, "no taxation without consent." The American

---

4. Frohnen, ed. *The American Republic: Primary Sources*, 92–7.

5. Frohnen, ed. *The American Republic: Primary Sources*, 98–100.

colonies weren't represented in Parliament; therefore, according to the principles of the Magna Carta and the Petition of Right, they could not be taxed.

In 1682, William Penn sailed to America to establish a colony called Pennsylvania. Before setting out for the new world Penn regularly found himself in trouble. As an outspoken Quaker with a fiery pen, he had sporadic run-ins with the religious authorities in England and was imprisoned for a time in the Tower of London. Quakers in general were a persecuted sect. Their property was regularly confiscated by the crown, and they occasionally lost their lives in their struggle against the "heresies" of the Church of England. Penn vigorously defended the Quaker religion but simultaneously championed religious toleration and the abolition of laws privileging one religious sect over another. Pennsylvania, under Penn's leadership, became a thriving colony characterized by religious tolerance.

In addition to leading the colony and planning its capitol, Philadelphia, Penn was a prolific writer whose essays on government and religious toleration were widely read. Like most American colonists until well into the eighteenth century, Penn thought of himself as an Englishman. When he thought of property, he thought in terms of the English common law stretching back through the Petition of Right to the Magna Carta. Penn insisted that it is the common law that "Fix[es] and Preserve[s] Property."[6] Property rights were possessed by Englishmen as an inheritance from the common law tradition. In a 1679 essay Penn summarizes the English system under three fundamental principles. The first is "Property, that is, Right and Title to your own Lives, Liberties, and Estates: In this, every Man is a Sort of Little Sovereign to himself: No Man has Power over his Person, to Imprison or hurt it, or over his Estate to Invade or Usurp it." But Penn also acknowledges that property can be forfeited. "Only your own Transgression of the Laws, (and those of your own making too) lays you open to Loss; which is but the Punishment due to your Offences." Yet even then there are limits to the taking, for the loss can only be "in Proportion to the Fault committed."[7] In placing property at the fore of his discussion, Penn makes clear his view that property "is the first and most fix'd Part of English Government."[8]

6. Penn, *The Political Writings of William Penn*, 54.
7. Penn, *The Political Writings of William Penn*, 386.
8. Penn, *The Political Writings of William Penn*, 237.

Note a couple of points: First, Penn does not argue in terms of a natural right to property, as John Locke would only a decade later. Instead, Penn thinks in terms of the rights and privileges of Englishmen. Second, he has an expansive understanding of property that includes life and liberty as well as physical property. As we will see, in the American colonies the word "property" is sometimes used in this expansive way and at other times it is more narrowly limited to tangible goods, with land representing the quintessential form. Finally, by listing property as the first fundamental principle of English government, Penn is asserting the connection between liberty and property. The liberties enjoyed by Englishmen as an inheritance are tied to the respect for private property. Implied in this assertion is the claim that when the king or parliament arbitrarily violate the private property of any one citizen, the liberties of all are put in jeopardy.

The Glorious Revolution of 1688 brought turmoil to the American colonies as well as a change in the English monarchy. James II sought to throw off the limitations imposed on his power by Parliament and the charters. He attempted to consolidate his power, ignored Parliament, and imprisoned those who opposed him. Angry citizens in Boston led an insurrection against the king and his authority. The leading men of the town drew up a declaration of grievances detailing the various ways the king and his men had abused their power. Included in the list is the claim that the king's appointed governor made laws and levied taxes "as he pleased"—which is to say, without consent. These English citizens in America had been informed by the king's men that "the people of New-England were all Slaves, and the only difference between them and Slaves is their not being bought and sold." Furthermore, the king's men insisted "that we must not think the Privileges of Englishmen would follow us to the end of the World: Accordingly, we have been treated with multiplied contradictions to Magna Carta, the rights of which we laid claim unto." Not only were taxes levied without the consent of the governed, "persons who did but peaceably object against the raising of Taxes without an Assembly, have been for it fined, some twenty, some thirty, and others fifty Pounds."[9]

But perhaps worst of all, the people's ownership of the land itself was denied. "We were every day told, That no man was owner of a Foot

9. Frohnen, ed. *The American Republic: Primary Sources*, 103.

of Land in all the Colony." It doesn't take much imagination to sense the righteous anger of those hard-working New Englanders when they were told that the land they had labored to subdue did not really belong to them. "Writs of Intrusion began every where to be served on People, that after all their Sweat and their Cost upon their formerly purchased Lands, thought themselves Free-holders of what they had. And the Governor caused the Lands pertaining to these and those Particular Men, to be measured out for his Creatures to take possession of; and the Right Owners, for pulling up the Stakes, have passed through Molestations enough to tire all the patience in the World."[10] The king's "creatures" indeed.

Back in England, James II fled the country, and William of Orange and his wife Mary (daughter of James II) were invited to take the throne with the condition that they agree to a document written by Parliament that has come to be called "The English Bill of Rights." That document served to establish once and for all the supremacy of Parliament. It also set out a detailed succession to the throne that excluded Catholics (James II was Catholic). Most significantly for our purposes it affirmed the inherited rights of Englishmen, including the principle that all laws, including laws to levy taxes, must have the consent of Parliament.

In the wake of the Glorious Revolution, John Locke's *Second Treatise on Civil Government* was published. It eventually made its way to the American colonies and influenced in important ways the debate about property. By the middle of the eighteenth century many writers in both England and America were thinking in terms of natural rights rather than (or at least in addition to) inherited English rights. The Lockean locution "life, liberty, and property" became ubiquitous in the American colonies.

By 1764 tensions between the American colonies and England were rising. Stephen Hopkins, then governor of Rhode Island (and later a signatory of the Declaration of Independence), published a pamphlet titled "The Rights of Colonies Examined." He begins with an appeal to the simple goodness of liberty: "Liberty is the greatest blessing that men enjoy, and slavery the heaviest curse that human nature is capable of." He goes on to admit, however, that "absolute liberty is, perhaps, incompatible with any kind of government."[11] Thus, effective government requires

---

10. Frohnen, ed. *The American Republic: Primary Sources*, 104.

11. Hyneman and Lutz, ed. *American Political Writings During the Founding Era*, 45.

that the absolute liberty of its citizens be curtailed, for the alternative is anarchy.

Hopkins extols the virtues of the English constitution, calling it "the best that ever existed among men." As evidence of the superiority of the English system, Hopkins points out that British subjects "are to be governed only agreeable to laws to which themselves have some way consented." Furthermore, they "are not to be compelled to part with their property but as it is called for by the authority of such laws." On the other hand, "those who are governed at the will of another, or of others, and whose property may be taken from them by taxes or otherwise without their own consent and against their will, are in the miserable condition of slaves."[12] Thus, liberty is the greatest blessing people can enjoy, and liberty only exists where citizens consent to the laws under which they live. More specifically, liberty exists where citizens' property can only be taken from them by their consent. Liberty and property are fundamentally intertwined. Without property, liberty is a façade, and without liberty, slavery is a fact.

As governor of Rhode Island, Hopkins was well-versed in the history of the English colonies in America. The Massachusetts colony and then Connecticut and Rhode Island were given charters by the king granting that the colonists and their children after them forever "should have and enjoy all the freedom and liberty that subjects in England enjoy; that they might make laws for their own government suitable to their circumstances, not repugnant to, but as near as might be agreeable to the laws of England; that they might purchase lands, acquire goods, and use trade for their advantage, and have an absolute property in whatever they justly acquired."[13] As with Locke, Penn, and the authors of Magna Carta, Hopkins believed that property and liberty were inseparable.

The Stamp Act of 1765 imposed a variety of new taxes upon the colonies. The colonists were furious. As a result, they convened the so-called Stamp Act Congress. The Congress issued a Declaration that begins, prudently enough, by expressing devotion and "warmest Sentiments of Affection and Duty to his Majesty's Person and Government." The colonists acknowledge that they are the subjects of the king and "owe the same

12. Hyneman and Lutz, ed. *American Political Writings During the Founding Era*, 46.

13. Hyneman and Lutz, ed. *American Political Writings During the Founding Era*, 47.

Allegiance to the Crown of Great-Britain, that is owing from his Subjects born within the Realm, and all due Submission to that August Body the Parliament of Great-Britain." The colonists still are the subjects of the king, and for that reason they "are entitled to all the inherent Rights and Liberties of his Natural born Subjects." The old principle, one that is now quite familiar to us, is reiterated: "It is inseparably essential to the Freedom of a People, and the undoubted Right of Englishmen, that no Taxes be imposed on them, but with their own Consent, given personally, or by their Representatives."

So far, so good. Nothing new here. But at this point the argument takes a turn that could only lead to more conflict. "The People of these Colonies are not, and from their local Circumstances cannot be, Represented in the House of Commons in Great-Britain."[14] Representation, so it was argued, requires some element of proximity. The vast expanse of the Atlantic separating the colonies from Parliament in London made it practically impossible for the colonists to be effectively represented in that body. Given the ancient principle we've been following, Parliament had no authority to levy taxes on the colonies, for the colonies were not represented and could never be represented there. The logic of the argument essentially removes the American colonies from the jurisdiction of Parliament.

Parliament repealed the Stamp Act only a year after passing it. The unrest in the colonies along with various boycotts of taxed goods cost England more revenue than the taxes generated. But lest the colonists get the impression that Parliament had rolled over, the same day the Stamp Act was repealed Parliament also issued "The Declaratory Act." In no uncertain terms it asserted that the colonies in America "are, and of right ought to be, subordinate unto, and dependent upon the imperial crown and parliament of Great Britain." Furthermore, it was asserted that the king *and* parliament "had, hath, and of right ought to have, full power and authority to make laws and statutes of sufficient force and validity to bind the colonies and people of America . . . in all cases whatsoever." And just to ensure that everything was covered, it was further declared that "all resolutions, votes, orders, and proceedings, in any of the said colonies or plantations, whereby the power and authority of the parliament of Great Britain, to make laws and statutes as aforesaid, is denied, or drawn into question, are, and are hereby declared to be, utterly null and void to

---

14. Frohnen, ed. *The American Republic: Primary Sources*, 117–18.

all intents and purposes whatsoever."[15] Needless to say, this only added fuel to the colonists' fire.

In the wake of the Stamp Act crisis, Providence lawyer Silas Downer delivered an address at the dedication of a tree of liberty. He begins not in the tone of a rebel but of a loyal subject: "We His Majesty's subjects, who live remote from the throne, and are inhabitants of a new world, are here met together to dedicate the Tree of Liberty." Downer acknowledges that he and his fellow countrymen "cheerfully recognize our allegiance to our sovereign Lord, George the third, King of Great-Britain," but that is where he draws the line. We "utterly deny any other dependence on the inhabitants of that island, than what is mutual and reciprocal between all mankind."[16] In other words, we are the king's loyal subjects, but Parliament has no authority over us.

Downer, like so many others during this tense time, recurs to the "principle universally agreed amongst us that they [parliament] cannot tax us, because we are not represented there."[17] Who, then, has the authority to tax the colonies? Obviously, the colonies themselves have that authority to the extent that consent can be obtained. As Downer puts it, "it hath been fully proved, and is a point not to be controverted, that in our constitution the having of property, especially landed estate, entitles the subject to a share in the government and framing of laws."[18]

Here is an important point. Ownership of property, especially land, justified participation in the legislative process. Why? The consent necessary to levy taxes must be given by those who will be taxed. Consent by propertyless people to tax those with property amounts to an unjust taking of property. Downer continues: "The Americans have such property and estate, but are not, and never can be represented in the British parliament. It is therefore clear that the assembly cannot pass any laws to bind us, but that we must be governed by our own parliaments, in which we can be in person, or by representation."[19] Note again the claim that the American colonies could not be represented in parliament. Notice further that the words "the Americans have such property and estate"

---

15. Frohnen, ed. *The American Republic: Primary Sources*, 135–6.

16. Frohnen, ed. *The American Republic: Primary Sources*, 140.

17. Frohnen, ed. *The American Republic: Primary Sources*, 141.

18. Frohnen, ed. *The American Republic: Primary Sources*, 142.

19. Frohnen, ed. *The American Republic: Primary Sources*, 142.

imply that property, especially in the form of land, was broadly distributed among the colonists. Americans were a propertied people.

But, one might ask: why all the fuss about taxes? Surely parliament was not threatening to appropriate all the possessions of the colonists. That, according to Downer, is not the point. There is a principle at the heart of the matter, and upon that principle turns the fact of liberty or the possibility of slavery. "If they can take one penny from us against our wills, they can take all. If they have such a power over our properties they must have proportionable power over our persons; and from hence it will follow, that they can demand and take away our lives, whensoever it shall be agreeable to their sovereign wills and pleasure."[20] Taxation without consent implies that every shred of property could be taken, but even more it implies an absolute control over a person, including control over life itself. The stakes, according to Downer, could not be higher.

The same sentiment is expressed in a 1775 sermon, published in Hartford, by Moses Mather titled "America's Appeal to the Impartial World." Mather appeals to the natural rights of the colonists as well as the rights derived from their affiliation with Britain. The question of taxation and consent is soon broached. Mather presents a stark dilemma: "the question is reduced to a single point, either the parliament hath no such power over the persons and properties of the Americans as is claimed, or the Americans are all slaves." Mather here makes the same move that Downer did. "Slavery consists in being wholly under the power and controul of another, as to our actions and properties: And he that hath authority to restrain and controul my conduct in any instance, without my consent, hath in all. And he that hath right to take one penny of my property, without my consent, hath right to take all."[21]

Mather urges his readers to fight, if necessary, in defense of "our country, our liberties and properties, ourselves and posterity." Such a struggle might cost much in terms of suffering and property. Lives would be lost. But even if all is forfeited to the cause, "compared with the prize at stake, our liberty, the liberty of our country, of mankind, and of millions yet unborn, it would be lighter than the dust on the balance: For if we submit, adieu for ever; adieu to property, for liberty will be lost, our only capacity for acquiring and holding property."[22]

20. Frohnen, ed. *The American Republic: Primary Sources*, 143.

21. Sandoz, ed. *Political Sermons of the American Founding Era*, 473–4.

22. Sandoz, ed. *Political Sermons of the American Founding Era*, 483.

Mather concludes with a flourish. He presents an idealized image of a nation characterized by peace, virtue, and property. "That government, in which the people are subject to no laws, or taxes, but by their voice or consent; condemned by no sentence but by the verdict of their equals; where property is near equally distributed; crimes clearly defined and distinguished; & punishments duly proportioned to their nature and magnitude; and where the rising generation are universally instructed in the principles of virtue, and the rudiments of government, there civil liberty & general public felicity, will flourish in the greatest perfection."[23] Mather imagines a virtuous society of propertied citizens where each person is capable of participating in the government because each owns property. In such a context, Mather sees the possibility for true happiness and lasting justice.

Future president, John Adams, in a 1775 letter to his wife Abigail, expresses his deep affection for New England, an "overweening prejudice . . . which I feel very often, and which, I fear, sometimes leads me to expose myself to just ridicule." He goes on to enumerate some of the advantages of New England, including "purer blood" [gulp], strong churches, good schools, and the township system of governing. He also includes property laws that provide for "a frequent division of landed property, and prevents monopolies of land."[24] Adams, however, is not naïve. He understands that liberty necessarily leads to inequality, and he even writes approvingly of a "natural aristocracy" of virtue and ability. He seems, though, to be making a distinction between a society characterized by broad ownership of property and a society where property is equally divided. The first is compatible with freedom and perhaps necessary for it. The second is incompatible with any workable, historically informed, or commonsense notion of liberty.

In an influential 1776 treatise titled "Thoughts on Government" Adams argues that the end of government is "the happiness of society." Happiness, in turn, "consists in virtue." Adams argues that, among other things, annual elections are an essential element of a free society, for they teach leaders "the great political virtues of humility, patience, and moderation, without which every man in power becomes a ravenous beast of prey." He goes on to recommend sumptuary laws, knowing that even the bare mention of such measures might "excite a smile." Nevertheless,

23. Sandoz, ed. *Political Sermons of the American Founding Era*, 492.
24. Adams to Abigail Adams, Oct. 29, 1775.

laws to prevent excessive displays of wealth necessarily imply a limitation on freedom generally and on the use of property more specifically. Of course, when Adams wrote, war with Britain was ongoing and such laws could provide revenue "sufficient to carry on this war forever." Yet he advocates sumptuary laws for times of peace as well. "Frugality is a great revenue, besides curing us of vanities, levities, and fopperies, which are real antidotes to all great, manly, and warlike virtues." Greatness requires restraint, and laws restricting excess spending and public displays of wealth can, according to Adams, help inculcate the habits that facilitate greatness.[25]

In a May 1776 letter to James Sullivan, Adams wrote, "Power always follows Property." This is an important point that Adams gleaned from the seventeenth-century English writer James Harrington. Adams continues: "The Ballance of Power in a Society, accompanies the Ballance of Property in Land. The only possible Way then of preserving the Ballance of Power on the side of equal Liberty and public Virtue, is to make the Acquisition of Land easy to every Member of Society: to make a Division of the Land into Small Quantities, So that the Multitude may be possessed of landed Estates. If the Multitude is possessed of the Ballance of real Estate, the Multitude will have the Ballance of Power, and in that Case the Multitude will take Care of the Liberty, Virtue, and Interest of the Multitude in all Acts of Government."[26] Obviously, if the principle holds today, the notion of property must extend beyond land. However, we should note that Adams recognizes the intimate connection between property, virtue, and political liberty. The three are, for Adams, inseparable, and anyone interested in creating a free society must attend to the issue of property ownership, for a nation of owners will possess the virtues necessary for self-government.

On July 4, 1776, representatives from the thirteen colonies issued the Declaration of Independence. By this time war had been raging for more than a year—that shot heard round the world was fired at Lexington on April 19, 1775. The Continental Congress assembled in Philadelphia determined that reconciliation with Britain was no longer desirable and perhaps not even possible. Thomas Jefferson was selected to chair a

25. Frohnen, ed. *The American Republic: Primary Sources*, 196–99.
26. Adams to James Sullivan, May 26, 1776.

committee to draft a document explaining to the world the reasons for the radical act of declaring independence.

The opening paragraphs of that document are familiar to all Americans. "We hold these truths to be self-evident, that all men are created equal, that they are endowed by their Creator with certain unalienable rights." This initial appeal to general principles couched in the rather abstract language of "Laws of Nature and of Nature's God" is followed by a bill of particulars that summarizes the specific "long train of abuses" the colonists had suffered. Unfortunately, this part of the document is not read nearly as much as the first two paragraphs, but it is equally important, for it is the accusation of tyranny that justifies severing ties with Britain. This list includes a variety of "abuses and usurpations" committed by the king. The focus is not the abuses of parliament, for as we have seen many colonists had long denied that parliament had any authority in the colonies. The colonists had, until this time, remained loyal to the king; therefore, a final separation required a specific separation from the Crown.

The accusations are briefly stated but clear enough to give readers a flavor of the abuses of power committed by King George. The king is accused of refusing "his Assent to Laws, the most welcome and necessary for the public good." He has "dissolved Representative Houses repeatedly, for opposing with manly firmness his invasions of the rights of the people." He has kept standing armies in times of peace and quartered troops in the homes of civilians. He has "plundered our seas, ravaged our Coasts, burnt our towns, and destroyed the lives of our people." Sandwiched between "cutting off our Trade with all parts of the world" and "depriving us in many cases, of the benefits of Trial by Jury" are seven brief words that, as we have seen, represent a long-standing and much-cherished principle that lies at the very heart of the colonists' notion of liberty: "For imposing taxes on us without our Consent."

The signatories of this document recognized the seriousness of their deed. If this enterprise failed and the war were lost, they would be hunted down and hanged as traitors. With the gravity of their actions permeating that hall in Philadelphia, they rose to affix their names to the parchment. The final sentence of the declaration summed up the hopes and prayers of those present: "And for the support of this Declaration, with a firm reliance on the protection of divine Providence, we mutually pledge to each other our Lives, our Fortunes and our sacred Honor."

Chapter Three

A Republic, If You Can Keep it

But they shall sit every man under his vine
and under his fig tree; and none shall make them afraid.

—MICAH 4:4

BY 1778 THE FATE of the thirteen colonies was still far from certain. In an attempt to better organize themselves to wage war, a confederation was formed. The document outlining this new relationship was called The Articles of Confederation. Under these articles, "Each State retains its sovereignty, freedom and independence." These independent states established a "firm league of friendship" for their "common defence, the security of their Liberties, and their mutual and general welfare." The several states committed to "assist each other, against all force offered to, or attacks made upon them."[1] Each state legislature, populated by representatives of the people, had exclusive authority to levy taxes on its citizens. Taxation or forfeitures of property were simply illegitimate apart from the consent of the proper representatives.

During the nine years that the Articles of Confederation were in force, state constitutions were written and debated. In Massachusetts, for example, a draft constitution was sent to the counties for comment. The leadership of Essex County replied with a detailed set of observations and recommendations that provide an interesting glimpse into the political

1. Frohnen, ed. *The American Republic: Primary Sources*, 200.

matters of the day. For our present purposes, the following sentence is of particular interest: "In a free government, a law affecting the person and property of its members, is not valid, unless it has the consent of the majority of the members, which majority should include those, who hold a major part of the property in the state."[2]

The Essex document proposes a bicameral legislature. Regarding the lower house—the house of representatives—"let regard be had only to the representation of persons, not of property." In this body, "the representatives are designed to represent the persons of the members, and therefore we do not consider a qualification in point of property necessary for them." The qualifications for the upper chamber—the senate—were different. "In electing the members of this body, let the representation of property be attended to." A minimum amount of property is suggested to qualify as an elector of senators. Thus, while the house of representatives represents the people of the state, the senate would represent the property of the state, "and no act will pass both branches of the legislative body, without having the consent of those members who hold a major part of the property in the state."[3] In sum, property may not be forfeited without the explicit consent of those who stand to lose it. This provision is an attempt to thwart those without property from unjustly taking the property of those who possess it.

In 1783 the war with Britain was successfully concluded. The colonies were now independent. By 1787 it was the general consensus that the Articles of Confederation required serious revision. The power of the central authority was woefully inadequate. Delegates were sent to Philadelphia to rework the document. They quickly agreed that the Articles should be scrapped and a new constitution written. After a long, hot summer of debate and compromise, the United States Constitution emerged. Like the Essex Report, the proposed constitution included a bicameral legislature composed of a senate and a house of representatives. Unlike the Essex proposal, the senate was not specifically tasked with representing property holders. Instead, each state legislature would choose two senators to represent the state's interests (this was, of course, changed by the Seventeenth Amendment, which stipulated that senators would henceforth be elected directly by the people). Members of the House of Representatives were (and still are) elected directly by the

2. Frohnen, ed. *The American Republic: Primary Sources*, 213.

3. Frohnen, ed. *The American Republic: Primary Sources*, 219–220.

people. In keeping with the principle that no taxes can be levied without the consent of the people, the House is responsible for originating all bills for raising revenue.

The new constitution was not universally embraced. The so-called Federalists supported ratification. The Anti-Federalists opposed it. Thoughtful and wise people were on both sides of this debate. Given the complexities and uncertainties of organizing a new government, this is not surprising. As Federalist Alexander Hamilton put it, the difficulty in such matters leads us to "see wise and good men on the wrong as well as on the right side of questions, of the first magnitude to society."[4] To this end, Hamilton proposed a series of papers to discuss the particulars of "the Plan" including the "security, which its adoption will afford to the preservation of that species of government [republicanism], to liberty and to property."[5] *The Federalist Papers,* penned by James Madison, Alexander Hamilton, and John Jay—and published under the pseudonym Publius— are the most famous collection of pamphlets championing ratification of the new constitution. In eighty-five essays, men who would become the fourth president, the first secretary of the treasury, and the first chief justice of the Supreme Court addressed a broad array of objections to the proposed constitution. Although the question of private property is not central to their immediate concerns, the topic is discussed on various occasions. While these references to property are mostly in passing, we can nevertheless glean some idea of how the authors thought about the topic.

In writing about the duration of the president's tenure in office, Hamilton recurs to a general principle that pertains primarily to property. "It is a general principle of human nature, that a man will be interested in whatever he possesses, in proportion to the firmness or precariousness of the tenure by which he holds it; will be less attached to what he holds by a momentary or uncertain title, than to what he enjoys by a title durable or certain; and, of course, will be willing to risk more for the sake of the one, than of the other."[6] The application of this principle to private property is obvious: Secure ownership fosters a long-term horizon of concern and helps to cultivate lines of affection across generations as property is tended with care and handed to one's descendants.

---

4. Carey and McClellan, ed. *The Federalist Papers,* No. 1, pg. 2.
5. Carey and McClellan, ed. *The Federalist Papers,* No. 1, pg. 4.
6. Carey and McClellan, ed. *The Federalist Papers,* No. 71, pg. 370.

Madison, in discussing the length of terms served by members of the Senate, argues that some duration in office is necessary to provide the stability that makes justice possible. "Rapid succession," even if the officials are decent and virtuous, will tend to introduce instability. The result of this instability will be the multiplication of laws intended to restore stability. But laws will be useless if they "be so voluminous that they cannot be read, or so incoherent that they cannot be understood: if they be repealed or revised before they are promulgated, or undergo such incessant changes, that no man who knows what the law is to-day, can guess what it will be to-morrow."[7] Anyone who has struggled through the labyrinthine IRS code, affixed a signature affirming that all the information is correct and lawful, and sent off his tax returns with fear and trembling knows precisely the evil Madison is talking about.

Madison continues by suggesting that unstable laws create an advantage for the "monied few" over the "industrious and uninformed mass of the people." As he puts it, "every new regulation concerning commerce or revenue, or in any manner affecting the value of the different species of property, presents a new harvest to those who watch the change, and can trace its consequences; a harvest, reared not by themselves, but by the toils and cares of the great body of their fellow citizens. This is a state of things in which it may be said, with some truth, that laws are made for the *few*, not for the *many*."[8] In other words, laws that create an advantage for the wealthy and disadvantage the poor are unjust and are a sign of public instability.

Perhaps the most famous of all the *Federalist Papers* is Number 10, in which Madison argues for the benefits of "an extended republic." There was considerable debate at the time whether a republic could exceed a certain very modest territorial size. The eighteenth-century French philosopher Montesquieu had argued that a republic must be relatively small or else forfeit its republican character. Montesquieu was widely read and appreciated in the American colonies. During the revolutionary period he was frequently quoted as an authority. Nevertheless, in *Federalist* 10, Madison breaks from Montesquieu on the subject of the extended republic.

In this essay, Madison addresses the issue of factions, which he defines as a group of citizens, either a majority or a minority, "who are united

7. Carey and McClellan, ed. *The Federalist Papers*, No. 62, pg. 323–4.

8. Carey and McClellan, ed. *The Federalist Papers*, No. 62, pg. 324.

and actuated by some common impulse of passion, or of interest, adverse to the rights of other citizens, or to the permanent and aggregate interests of the community."[9] Because minority factions can be controlled by "the republican principle," majority factions are Madison's primary concern. (In terms of my argument, a proletarian majority perfectly fits Madison's definition of faction.) Contrary to Montesquieu, Madison argues that a small republic is actually more susceptible to factions of the majority, for the small population and territory make it easier for a faction to achieve a majority and to act in concert. Madison argues that in a large republic majority factions will be less likely to form; and even if a majority exists, communication and organization will be rendered exceedingly difficult, given the land mass encompassed by the nation (Madison, of course, did not anticipate cable television, the internet, and Facebook).

According to Madison, "the most common and durable source of factions, has been the various and unequal distribution of property."[10] This being the case, one might think that Madison would suggest ways of eliminating inequalities of property. He does not, for the causes of faction "are thus sown in the nature of man."[11] To seek to remedy the problem of faction by eliminating their cause would be fatal to liberty. Thus, Madison asserts that those who rage for "an equal division of property" pursue an "improper" and "wicked project."[12] Yet Madison is writing at a time when the vast majority of his audience consisted of small-scale property holders. The majority of Americans were propertied, though their properties were by no means equal.

Although Madison broke with him on the question of the proper size of a republic, Montesquieu cast a long shadow over America's founding generation. His discussion of equality and property in a republic merits our attention, for whether particular Americans ultimately agreed or disagreed with him on this matter, his views were well known, highly regarded, and influential. It is safe to say that Montesquieu's arguments played a significant role in framing the debate about equality, liberty, and property.

9. Carey and McClellan, ed. *The Federalist Papers*, No. 10, pg. 43.
10. Carey and McClellan, ed. *The Federalist Papers*, No. 10, pg. 44.
11. Carey and McClellan, ed. *The Federalist Papers*, No. 10, pg. 43.
12. Carey and McClellan, ed. *The Federalist Papers*, No. 10, pg. 48.

According to Montesquieu, a republic is constituted by the love for democracy, which is constituted by love for equality and (perhaps surprisingly) frugality, both of which must be cultivated by the laws. Virtue is the indispensable key to a healthy republic, and this virtue is encapsulated in "love of the laws and the homeland."[13] Montesquieu's ideal republic consists of men of "middling talents and fortunes." A republic of "many middling people" can be soberly governed and happy to the degree that the people are sober and happy.[14] In order to prevent harmful inequalities from entering the republic and destroying it, Montesquieu advocates the regulation of "dowries, gifts, inheritances, testaments, in sum, all the kinds of contracts. For if it were permitted to give one's goods to whomever one wanted" the "fundamental laws" of the state would be altered.[15] Americans had always rejected the idea of primogeniture and laws of entail, and to that extent they follow Montesquieu. The vast majority stopped, however, from suggesting that explicit legal limits should be placed on gifts and inheritances.

Montesquieu is not agitating for complete or perfect equality. He is, though, arguing that a republic must be comprised of "middling people" in possession of middling property, else vast differences will destroy the fundamental unity of the state. The scale of property matters. As he puts it, "it is not sufficient in a good democracy for the portions of land to be equal; they must be small."[16] To this end, he suggests efforts that "reduce differences or fix them at a certain point; after which, it is the task of particular laws to equalize inequalities, so to speak, by the burdens they impose on the rich and the relief they afford to the poor."[17] It is fair to assume that some form of taxation is at least one avenue he has in mind. Furthermore, it is crucial to note that he advocates reducing differences or fixing differences within certain parameters. He is not suggesting the possibility of rendering all property equal, but he is certainly in favor of governmental action to reduce inequality.

Montesquieu continues by admitting that a republic "founded on commerce" could very well include individuals of great wealth whose "mores are not corrupted." How can this be? "The spirit of commerce

---

13. Montesquieu, *The Spirit of the Laws*, 36.

14. Montesquieu, *The Spirit of the Laws*, 44.

15. Montesquieu, *The Spirit of the Laws*, 45.

16. Montesquieu, *The Spirit of the Laws*, 47.

17. Montesquieu, *The Spirit of the Laws*, 47.

brings with it the spirit of frugality, economy, moderation, work, wisdom, tranquility, order, and rule. Thus, as long as the spirit of commerce continues to exist, the wealth it produces has no bad effect." The problem comes when "an excess of wealth destroys the spirit of commerce."[18] Frugality is necessary, and Montesquieu does not hesitate to recommend sumptuary laws to aid in the restraint that frugality requires. When the positive benefits of commerce are undermined by a spirit of luxury, the inequalities that were tolerable and even beneficial become vicious and destructive of the soul of the republic. As Montesquieu puts it, "so far as luxury is established in a republic, so far does the spirit turn to the interest of the individual," and notions of the common good or the glory of the state fall to the wayside. "A soul corrupted by luxury has many other desires; soon it becomes an enemy of the laws that hamper it."[19] Thus, great differences of wealth, generated by commerce, can give birth to the spirit of luxury, which undermines the republic and chafes against its laws, for law represents limits and restraint—and the soul given over to the pursuit of luxury is one that abhors limits.

While he argues that equality is essential for the health of the republic, Montesquieu identifies another danger, namely, the desire for absolute equality. He understands that liberty, as well as natural differences, will lead to inequalities among citizens. These differences will manifest themselves not only in terms of property but also in terms of citizenship. The spirit of inequality will lead to aristocracy, and the spirit of extreme equality will lead to the despotism of one. Thus, "the principle of democracy is corrupted not only when the spirit of equality is lost but also when the spirit of extreme equality is taken up."[20] Montesquieu insists that "as far as the sky is from the earth, so far is the true spirit of equality from the spirit of extreme equality."[21] The spirit of extreme equality seeks to obliterate all differences of property and station, thus undermining respect for authority and dissolving public order. Social corruption will ensue. "The people will distribute among themselves all the public funds; and, just as they will join the management of business to their laziness, they will want to join the amusements of luxury to their poverty. But given their

18. Montesquieu, *The Spirit of the Laws*, 48.

19. Montesquieu, *The Spirit of the Laws*, 98.

20. Montesquieu, *The Spirit of the Laws*, 112.

21. Montesquieu, *The Spirit of the Laws*, 114.

laziness and their luxury, only the public treasure can be their object."[22]
This amounts to bread and circuses on the public's dime although, in
today's dollars, that amounts to trillions.

Thus, both the spirit of extreme equality as well as the spirit of
inequality must be guarded against, and laws must be erected to help
preserve the kind of equality that fosters a vibrant republic. The founders
seem to be aware of both dangers. When Madison insists that attempting to effect "an equal division of property" is "wicked," we can see him
rejecting the dangers of extreme equality. Yet, at the same time, when
partisans from both the Federalists and the Anti-Federalists champion
the broad distribution of property, we can see them as attacking the evils
of inequality and seeking to maintain a vibrant middle class. Striking a
balance between both extremes is one of the challenges besetting any
republic.

Let us return now to the ratification debates. Noah Webster, the same
Webster who compiled the first American dictionary, was an ardent
champion of the Constitution. In the fall of 1787 he published a pamphlet titled "Leading Principles of the Constitution" in which he provides a detailed discussion of the proposed document. Interspersed in
that discussion is an argument about the necessary relationship between
property and freedom. He takes issue with Montesquieu, who insisted
on the primacy of virtue, and argues that well-distributed property is the
only means to secure freedom: "the system of the great Montesquieu will
ever be erroneous, till the words *property or lands in fee simple* are sub-
stituted for *virtue*, throughout his *Spirit of the Laws*." As Webster puts it,
real power consists in nothing other than the ownership of property. He
notes that the history of England is largely a story of the struggle of the
people against the nobility, and "we observe that the power of the people
has increased in an exact proportion to their acquisitions of property."
In fact, "a general and tolerably equal distribution of landed property is
the whole basis of national freedom."[23] Webster's "tolerable" equality suggests not the "extreme equality" feared by Montesquieu but a society of
"middling" property holders who find their power and unity in property
ownership—citizens with enough property to be independent but who
do not possess so much as to be a menace to others.

22. Montesquieu, *The Spirit of the Laws*, 113.

23. Frohnen, ed. *The American Republic: Primary Sources*, 293. Italics in original.

Webster argues that the traditionally asserted bulwarks of freedom—freedom of the press, trial by jury, habeas corpus, as well as bills of rights—"are all inferior considerations, when compared with a general distribution of real property among every class of people."[24] Consolidation of real property, through inheritance laws and entailments, are "more dangerous to liberty and republican government, than all the constitutions that can be written on paper, or even than a standing army." Ultimately, for Webster, a well-informed, propertied populace is the foundation undergirding a free society. Thus, "liberty stands on the immoveable basis of a general distribution of property and diffusion of knowledge."[25] A society of poorly educated and propertyless citizens would, in Webster's mind, threaten the very existence of the republic. In short, Webster fears a proletarian citizenry with little knowledge of history and little sense of civic duty. Such a class of citizens would be ripe for a demagogue or primed to fall for the lavish promises of socialist dreamers.

Anti-Federalists opposed the ratification of the proposed constitution for a variety of reasons, most of which centered on the fear that the plan provided too many avenues for the consolidation of power. The Anti-Federalists argued that, among other things, the "necessary and proper" clause of the Constitution was too broad, that the three branches of government were not sufficiently separated, and many found the initial absence of a bill of rights objectionable. Some also followed Montesquieu in arguing that a republic must be relatively small and, as a consequence, the extended republic proposed by the Constitution was incompatible with liberty. Concerning property, one writer using the pseudonym Centinel asserts that "a republican, or free government, can only exist where the body of the people are virtuous, and where property is pretty equally divided." Where this condition is ignored or forfeited, "the nature of the government is changed, and an aristocracy, monarchy or despotism will rise on its ruin."[26] Again, "pretty equally divided" seems to attempt the same balance struck by Montesquieu between extreme equality and inequality.

A subtler argument turns on the question of representation. Another Anti-Federalist, Brutus, begins by claiming that "the authority to lay

24. Frohnen, ed. *The American Republic: Primary Sources*, 293.

25. Frohnen, ed. *The American Republic: Primary Sources*, 295.

26. Storing, ed. *The Anti-Federalist*, 16.

and collect tax is the most important of any power that can be granted."[27]
As we have seen, the idea of taxation is inseparable in the American mind
from the idea of consent, which is made possible through representatives. Thus, "when a government is to receive its support from the aid
of the citizens, it must be so constructed as to have the confidence, respect, and affection of the people."[28] But when a republic consists of such
great tracts of land and varied cultural regions, the legislature is far less
likely to enjoy the confidence, respect, and affection of the people, for
"the confidence which the people have in their rulers, in a free republic,
arises from their knowing them, from their being responsible to them for
their conduct, and from the power they have of displacing them when
they misbehave."[29] In an extended republic, "the people in general would
be acquainted with very few of their rulers: the people at large would
know little of their proceedings, and it would be extremely difficult to
change them." Brutus predicts a troubling situation in which the people
are so distant from their representatives that they cannot monitor them
with any degree of effectiveness. "In so great a republic, the great officers
of government would soon become above the controul of the people,
and abuse their power to the purpose of aggrandizing themselves, and
oppressing them."[30] Brutus is warning that a large republic could pave
the way for the emergence of a plutocratic class. In such circumstances,
the consent of the people is muted and perhaps meaningless. Without
consent, taxation represents an illegitimate action violating a basic principle extending far back into American and English history. Consent,
through representation, requires a scale that facilitates interaction with
one's representative. When that scale is exceeded, real representation is
jeopardized and with it legitimate consent. In such a context, property is
endangered and with it freedom.

By 1790, all thirteen colonies had ratified the new Constitution. Because
he served as minister to France from 1785 to 1789, Thomas Jefferson
did not attend the Philadelphia convention or actively participate in the
ratification debates. He was, though, kept informed of events in the colonies by his protégé, James Madison, with whom he maintained a lively

27. Storing, ed. *The Anti-Federalist*, 111.

28. Storing, ed. *The Anti-Federalist*, 115.

29. Storing, ed. *The Anti-Federalist*, 115–16.

30. Storing, ed. *The Anti-Federalist*, 116.

correspondence. In a 1785 letter to Madison, Jefferson discusses the importance of property. Jefferson notes that when he first arrived in France, he took a walk to familiarize himself with the countryside. He soon fell in with "a poor woman," and "wishing to know the condition of the labouring poor I entered into conversation with her." She told of her difficulty finding work, the abysmal wages on offer for a day laborer, and the days she could afford no food at all. As they parted, Jefferson gave her the equivalent of three day's wages. "She burst into tears of a gratitude which I could perceive was unfeigned, because she was unable to utter a word. She had probably never before received so great an aid." This encounter led Jefferson to reflect on the issue of property and the "unequal division" that existed in France and all over Europe.

"I am conscious," Jefferson admits, "that an equal division of property is impracticable." Nevertheless, "enormous inequality" is the cause of such misery, and the suffering is such that "legislators cannot invent too many devices for subdividing property, only taking care to let their subdivisions go hand in hand with the natural affections of the human mind." Eliminating laws of primogeniture and entail are one remedy for this vexing problem. "Another means of silently lessening the inequality of property is to exempt all from taxation below a certain point, and to tax the higher portions of property in geometrical progression as they rise." Ultimately, Jefferson voices his commitment to a propertied citizenry: "It is not too soon to provide by every possible means that as few as possible shall be without a little portion of land. The small landholders are the most precious part of a state."[31]

Madison's reflections on property exhibit elements of Locke, but his debt to Jefferson is also clear. Writing in 1792, Madison offers a fairly standard definition of property as "that dominion which one man claims and exercises over the external things of the world, in exclusion of every other individual." More broadly, property "embraces every thing to which a man may attach a value and have a right; and *which leaves to every one else the like advantage.*" Land, money, or other tangible goods constitute property, but additionally, "a man has a property in his opinions and the free communication of them." Thus, a person, according to Madison, has property in his thoughts, opinions, and choices. He summarizes this expansive definition of property: "In a word, as a man is said to have a right to his property, he may be equally said to have a property in his rights."

31. Jefferson, *The Works of Thomas Jefferson*, vol. VIII, 194–6.

Following Locke and virtually every prominent thinker of the American founding, Madison argues that the purpose of government is, at least in part, to "protect property of every sort." A government is just to the extent that it protects property and is unjust to the degree that it fails to do so.[32]

In the same year, while considering the problem of political parties, Madison reflects on the problem of inequality in property and strikes a Jeffersonian tone in the remedies he proposes. Madison is convinced that political parties are simply unavoidable. There are strategies, however, to blunt the dangers inherent in the spirit of party. These include "establishing political equality among all" and "withholding unnecessary opportunities from a few, to increase the inequality of property, by an immoderate, and especially unmerited, accumulation of riches." Alluding to Jefferson's suggestion that the tax structure could "silently" reduce inequalities of property, Madison argues that inequalities can be remedied "by the silent operation of laws, which, without violating the rights of property, reduce extreme wealth towards a state of mediocrity, and raise extreme indigence towards a state of comfort."[33] It is reasonable to assume that these "silent operations" of Madison are the same as the "means of silently lessening the inequality of property" suggested by Jefferson. It is clear that neither is advocating absolute equality. Instead, both are concerned with extreme inequalities that would weaken the fiber of the republic. Again, Montesquieu's delicate balance appears to be the goal.

In sum, leading figures of the Revolutionary generation, Federalists and Anti-Federalists alike, were convinced that a republic can only exist if a vast majority of citizens are middle-class property owners. No one agitated for absolute equality of property, for they believed that liberty and inequality of property go hand-in-hand. At the same time, they were egalitarian enough to be suspicious of great accumulations of wealth that produce broad class distinctions. Surely one of the most frightening prospects for the founders would have been a large class of citizens altogether bereft of property.

By property they meant primarily, but not exclusively, *land*. A propertied citizenry was essential to the health of the republic, and given the broad distribution of land at the time of the American founding, the

---

32. Madison, *The Writings of James Madison*, vol. 6, 101–3. Italics in original.
33. Madison, *The Writings of James Madison*, vol. 6, 86.

framers of the Constitution had good reason to hope that, with vigilance, liberty could be sustained.

These founding fathers of the American republic understood that a large class of propertyless citizens, if they possessed the franchise, would be a danger to the very survival of the republic, for they would have every incentive to vote advantages to themselves at the expense of the propertied few. In so doing, a fundamental principle, expressed in the Magna Carta and affirmed throughout English and American history would be blatantly violated. The principle "no taxation without consent" implied that taxes could only be levied on those who both own property and consent to the taxation. Such a claim seems to suggest that only those who possess property should enjoy the right to participate in the legislative process. In the early days of the republic, the vast majority of citizens belonged to the class of "middling" property owners, so each individual had a stake in the republic. Those without property aspired to rise to that level and thus already thought like property owners. Today the middle class is shrinking, and we are left with a question: Can the republic the Founders created exist with a proletarian majority? The Founders would have been deeply skeptical. If the American republic was founded by and for a propertied people, the diminishment of a propertied citizenry will consequently usher in something fundamentally different from the republic envisioned by those who founded it.

Today Plutocratic Socialism represents this altered vision of the American future. The dynamics that have brought us to this crossroads are complex, but the general contours are clear. When a plutocratic class makes laws to advance itself and its interests at the expense of those without substantial wealth, there will eventually be a reaction. When the majority of citizens have been proletarianized, they will, if they are molded into a unified political movement, demand policies that direct government services toward themselves. Opportunists will recognize the potential for a realignment of power by exploiting the grievances of the propertyless. Today the only way the plutocrats can maintain their power is to pretend to side with the Woke Socialists by employing the language of social justice, giving the Woke leaders a platform, and using political and economic concessions to mollify the mob.

In the name of socialism (wrapped in the cloak of social justice and climate fears) the Woke Socialists are seeking a dramatic expansion of power that will, so they assure us, usher in a better world characterized by equality, democracy, and justice. Unlike the founders of our Republic, these new idealists talk more about equality than about freedom, they talk more about rights than about duties, and they talk more about government services than about property. This shift highlights a fundamental principle that virtually all of the Founders grasped with absolute clarity and that is rapidly receding from our sight: Freedom and private property stand or fall together.

Chapter Four

Challenges to Property
Revolutions Political and Industrial

> But this natural harmony could endure only so long as the
> material conditions of life stretched in an uninterrupted chain
> from the highest to the lowest, a chain in which the various
> links were not too far apart. It was utterly destroyed when there
> came to be at one end of the social ladder a disinherited mass,
> and at the other an insolent plutocracy.
>
> —BERTRAND DE JOUVENEL

THE YEARS 1789–1848 WERE fertile times for revolutionary thought and action. From the storming of the Bastille in 1789 to the publication of the *Communist Manifesto* in 1848—along with the political unrest of that year—a revolutionary tide swept Europe. In this context it is important to recognize that the American "Revolution" is misnamed. It was, properly speaking, a War for Independence whereby the colonists forcefully separated from British rule. However, the colonists had no intention of fundamentally transforming society, which is precisely the goal of truly revolutionary thought. One of the key aims of both the French Revolution and the various communist revolutions was the transformation of property ownership. In many ways, the Industrial Revolution accomplished a transformation no less dramatic. It is important to attend to both kinds of revolution—political and industrial—to understand property today and to grasp the context out of which Plutocratic Socialism emerges.

Rousseau and the French Revolution

At the same time that Americans were forging their new constitutional order grounded, as we have seen, in a deep respect for private property, a revolution was brewing in France that took a decidedly different course. The pragmatic Americans harbored no illusions about creating a perfect society. They did, however, think they could do better than the Articles of Confederation. Hence, they sought to form "a more perfect union," an improvement on the current state of affairs but one firmly rooted in reality. They had no aspirations to form a utopian paradise. On the other hand, the leaders of the French revolution were disciples of Rousseau, who once frankly informed a guest: "Sir, I have no liking for the world. I live here in a world of fantasies, and cannot tolerate the world as it is… Mankind disgusts me."[1] It is said that Robespierre reread Rousseau's *Social Contract* every day.[2]

Rousseau was a flamboyant and unorthodox individual who in his autobiography boasted that "I am not made like anyone I am acquainted with, perhaps like no one in existence." He continues by declaring that after he was made, nature broke the mold. He was, he insisted, one of a kind.[3] Like other social contract thinkers, Rousseau begins his reflections on politics by positing a pre-political state of nature, but unlike many, he is more candid about the historical reality of this state. Rousseau notes that previous state-of-nature theorists had never thought to question the historical reality of the state of nature, even though he admits Holy Scripture teaches that such a state never existed. Nevertheless, as he begins his discourse on how inequality could have emerged from an original equality, Rousseau sweeps aside all appeals to history. "Let us therefore begin by putting aside all the facts, for they have no bearing on the question." He boldly implores his readers to heed his conjectures: "here is your history, as I have thought to read it, not in the books of your fellowman, who are liars, but in nature, who never lies."[4]

1. Quoted in Pipes, *Property and Freedom*, 39.
2. Pipes, *Property and Freedom*, 42.
3. Rousseau, *The Confessions of Jean Jacques Rousseau*, vol. 1, 1.
4. Rousseau, *The Basic Political Writings*, 46.

Rousseau then embarks on a detailed description of life in an imagined state of nature where everyone is absolutely free and absolutely equal. It is Rousseau who propagates the myth of the so-called "noble savage," who enjoys a healthy and vibrant life without care. He is a solitary creature who does not worry about the morrow, who eats when he is hungry, and sleeps when he is tired. If he happens to encounter a female who catches his fancy, a night of sexual pleasure might ensue, but in the morning he will wander off in search of food or whatever else captures his attention. Rationality is not something that this "noble" creature possesses, for rationality leads only to dissatisfaction, inordinate desires, and worry about the future. In such a state, freedom is absolute and all are perfectly equal.

According to Rousseau, "the first person who, having enclosed a plot of land, took it into his head to say *this is mine* and found people simple enough to believe him, was the true founder of civil society."[5] Private property, then, is the essential foundation of society. Private property also introduces the possibility, and very soon the reality, of inequality. Owners of property ceased their wandering and settled in one place. They sought to expand their holdings and began to think about the future. With this change, labor—something previously unheard of—emerges, men became civilized, and the human race was, according to Rousseau, ruined. Thus, the freedom and equality that were perfectly enjoyed in the state of nature are replaced by the slavery of labor and the inequality that invariably emerges with private property.

Rousseau's *Social Contract* (the book favored by Robespierre) attempts to develop a political program for restoring the freedom and equality originally enjoyed in the state of nature. Rousseau observes that in the contemporary world of private property and political authority "man is born free, and everywhere he is in chains."[6] Given this deplorable state of human affairs, is there any way to recapture the happiness that was forfeited by leaving the state of nature and descending into society? Rousseau does not think humans can return to that pristine original state. Once the apple has been eaten, there is no going back. Yet he is hopeful that, given the right program, freedom and equality can be reborn in an even higher and more perfect condition than that which existed in the state of nature.

---

5. Rousseau, *The Basic Political Writings*, 69.
6. Rousseau, *The Basic Political Writings*, 156.

The key to his program is the mysterious "general will," which represents the will of all people if, in fact, everyone knew and pursued that which was truly best. Of course, not everyone is enlightened enough to subordinate his individual desires to the general will. Thus, to keep this notion from being an empty shell, Rousseau boldly asserts that "whoever refuses to obey the general will will be forced to do so by the entire body. This means merely that he will be forced to be free."[7] A curious notion of freedom, to be sure, but it is not indefensible, for in Rousseau's conceptualization the general will is infallible. Thus, in a convoluted fashion, all are free even if some must be compelled to that end.

Rousseau's radical notion of solidarity among citizens implies that private property holdings are valid only to the extent that they benefit the whole. He asserts that "every man by nature has a right to everything he needs," yet because ownership is facilitated, ratified, and defended by the state, "owners are considered trustees of the public good." It follows that "each private individual's right to his very own store is always subordinate to the community's right to all."[8] In this way equality is recovered, for each individual is equally part of the general will, and ownership is merely a convention that is subordinate to the needs of all. It doesn't take much reflection to see that in Rousseau's brave new world freedom has nothing to do with individual liberty, and private property is an illusion.

Rousseau's writings were formative in the thinking of those who led the French Revolution, and one of the best contemporary critics of that political debacle was Edmund Burke. Burke wrote his *Reflections on the Revolution in France* during the early stages of the revolution. He predicted with uncanny prescience the frenzied wave of destruction that would fall over that troubled land. According to Burke, legitimate freedom is always qualified by responsibility and tempered by prudence. Furthermore, true freedom cannot exist without a healthy respect for private property, and jettisoning property rights could only end in chaos and bloodshed. Yet the existence of a system that respects private property is one where material equality is simply impossible.[9] Thus, contrary to the fevered dreams of Rousseau, who imagined a world of perfect freedom and perfect equality, Burke argues that both ideals limit and qualify each other. True freedom requires the possibility of some inequalities, for true

---

7. Rousseau, *The Basic Political Writings*, 167.

8. Rousseau, *The Basic Political Writings*, 168–9.

9. Burke, *Reflections on the Revolution in France*, 141–3.

freedom is founded in property ownership and the possibility of property exchange. At the same time, a society of property owners shares an equal status as owners even if the amount of property differs. This equality of status facilitates a healthy and vibrant freedom.

With the spirit of Rousseau hovering over the French Revolution, it is not difficult to see how this revolution differed from the one in America. Rousseau's dissatisfaction with the world leads him to create, *ex nihilo* as it were, a utopian social and political vision that was only tangentially connected to reality. Where the American founders were by and large men of political experience, Rousseau had no political responsibilities and was therefore unconstrained by hard facts. Where the American founders tended to view human nature through a traditional Christian lens that affirms the notion of Original Sin, Rousseau argued that men in their original state were innocent, free, and equal, and only with the introduction of property did avarice, inequality, and servitude enter the world. Furthermore, the notion of Original Sin informs the understanding of power developed by Madison and others. Madison argued that power tends to expand and consolidate, and centralized power increases both the opportunity for abuse as well as the scale of potential abuses. On the other hand, Rousseau offers his social contract, oriented to and governed by the infallible general will. An infallible power is not one to be feared; rather, it should be embraced, and good citizens will make every effort to eradicate impediments to the all-knowing and absolute central power. For the Americans, private property was an essential social and political institution, and property rights were seen as bulwarks against the encroachments of the state. For Rousseau, private property is held merely at the pleasure of the state and can be seized by the state at any time for any cause. Of course, if the state is infallible, there is nothing to worry about. History has proven otherwise.

The French Revolution pitted the agitated intellectual classes and the down-trodden citizens against what was in many instances a debased and decadent aristocracy. To the extent that aristocrats failed to do justice to those entrusted to their care, the dissatisfaction of the people was warranted. To the extent that the intellectual leaders of the revolution were politically inexperienced ideologues bent on remaking French society from the ground up, the Reign of Terror was shaping up in the wings long before the blood began to flow in the streets.

It is important to note that the French National Assembly affirmed the sanctity of natural rights, and the constitution adopted in 1793 stated that equality, liberty, security, and property were fundamental and in-alienable rights of men.[10] Yet despite these declarations, the revolution-aries did not consistently respect property rights. It seems one can pursue perfect equality or perfect liberty, but not both. Perfect equality is in-compatible with property rights, and perfect liberty is incompatible with perfect equality. This being the case, Rousseau's project to achieve perfect equality and perfect liberty was doomed from the start, unless, of course, he redefined liberty in a way that made it compatible with equality but simultaneously unrecognizable. This he did. In the process, the right to private property was destroyed. When the principles of Rousseau were applied, the ensuing revolution paved the way for Napoleon.

Marx and the Industrial Revolution

While political revolution was churning in France, another kind of revo-lution was taking place in England. Steam power and machine technol-ogy gave birth to a revolution in industry. At the same time, and for a variety of reasons, common land in England was being privatized via the so-called Enclosure Movement, thus greatly reducing the amount of land available to the small landless farmer, who formerly could graze livestock on common land. The Enclosure Acts gave birth to a new labor pool, and the new factories provided ample employment opportunities for those recently deprived of access to common lands.

The results, at least in the short-term, were mixed. The indepen-dence that farming, even on common lands, afforded was exchanged for a steady paycheck that was often barely adequate. Because factory work often required repetitive movement rather than sheer physical strength, both men and women could work in the factories. However, this shift doubled the labor pool, driving the cost of labor down and often making it necessary for both wives and husbands to work. The same logic also opened the door for children to enter the workforce.

In the early nineteenth century, a group of protesters, calling them-selves Luddites, took measures into their own hands. Concerned that the new textile manufacturing processes were depriving them of jobs and therefore of livelihoods, Luddites took to smashing the large-frame weaving machines they believed were responsible for their troubles. After the leaders were caught and hung, the movement lost its momentum;

10. French Republic Constitution of 1793. Paragraph 122.

however, the sentiment, if not the active destruction of machines, persisted in some quarters as England endured the upheavals of the early Industrial Revolution.

Karl Marx (born 1818) saw the displacement of workers and abysmal wages as permanent features of the capitalist system. He lamented the deplorable conditions under which so many labored in "the dark, Satanic mills," as William Blake called them. He argued that capitalism would steadily diminish the worker, alienating him both from himself and from his labor and maintaining him at a point just this side of starvation. Anticipating the pitiful Okies immortalized in John Steinbeck's *The Grapes of Wrath* or the Lithuanian immigrants in Upton Sinclair's *The Jungle*, Marx argued that the bourgeoisie would hold the proletariat in virtual slavery: wage slavery, yes, but effective slavery nonetheless. This condition would fester until a critical mass of workers recognized their power, threw off their chains, overturned the capitalist system, and appropriated the means of production while abolishing the institution of private property. His clarion call, "Working men of all countries, unite!"[11] was intended to spark a world-wide revolution of the workers against their capitalist masters. In the wake of this uprising, Marx imagined a worker's paradise, where private property—specifically the means of production—was communally owned and where people would be provided for out of the common store of goods created by the common labor of all: from each according to his ability, to each according to his needs. But as with Rousseau and the French Revolutionaries, Marx's dream of a better world failed to materialize. In fact, as the twentieth century so painfully taught us, the worker's paradise seems an elusive dream requiring ever more government centralization and intervention, not to mention untold misery for the common man, the purported beneficiary. Utopias don't come cheap, nor, it would seem, do they come quickly.

Marx failed to anticipate a future where the market could create a situation in which wage laborers no longer suffered under the crushing fear and despondency of near starvation but could live lives of relative comfort and security. This turn of events would not have pleased him, for it's difficult to stimulate revolutionary fervor in workers who are comfortable. Yet, despite the unimpressive track record of the Marxist politicians and movements, rising inequality, nagging insecurity, and historical ignorance has today stimulated a resurgence of Marxist ideals.

11. Marx, *The Marx-Engels Reader*, 500.

Despite its colossal historic failures, Marx's analysis does get one thing right. He understood that those who attempt to remain aloof from capitalist modes of production—what we call today "economies of scale"—tend to be consumed. As Marx puts it, "the middle class—the small tradespeople, shopkeepers, and retired tradesmen generally, the handicraftsmen and peasants—all these sink gradually into the proletariat, partly because their diminutive capital does not suffice for the scale on which Modern Industry is carried on, and is swamped in the competition with the large capitalists."[12] Marx understood that human scale is tied to human flourishing. Today it is all too often the case that the small proprietors are disadvantaged while the large corporations reap the benefits secured by virtue of their size and, consequentially, their political influence.

As a result of the economic and political power of large-scale industry, property would be increasingly concentrated into fewer and fewer hands. The proletariat class would expand with the concentration of property. A decentralized economy comprised of small farms, artisans, and craftsmen is incompatible with an economy built around large-scale production, distribution, and consumption. Thus, "the bourgeoisie keeps more and more doing away with the scattered state of the population, of the means of production, and of property. It has agglomerated population, centralized means of production, and has concentrated property in a few hands. The necessary consequences of this was political centralization."[13] Marx understood that large scale industry and big government arise in tandem, feed off each other, and perpetuate each other. He understood that the concentration of capital—which is to say economic power— would lead to a concentration of political power.

There are, of course, social and political consequences to the concentration of property. It seems clear that as the population becomes increasingly proletarianized, it becomes increasingly less secure and naturally enjoins the creation and expansion of the welfare state. In other words, a proletarian society structured around democratic political forms will come to demand a strong, centralized state that is better equipped to satisfy the demands of a dependent, propertyless population. The first step in Marx's revolutionary program is "to raise the proletariat to the position of ruling class, to win the battle of democracy." The battle

12. Marx, *The Marx-Engels Reader*, 479–80.
13. Marx, *The Marx-Engels Reader*, 477.

of democracy is won at the ballot box when the proletarian class and its sympathizers can muster a majority. Once this is done, "the proletariat will use its political supremacy to wrest, by degrees, all capital from the bourgeoisie, to centralize all instruments of production in the hands of the State."[14]

However, history has clearly shown that the dictatorship of the working class never materializes. The revolution is invariably hijacked by a plutocratic minority intent on securing power and wealth. Thus the revolution is not simply fostered by a power-hungry tyrant or a cabal of wealthy aristocrats. Rather, when the proletarian class represents a majority of the voters, the revolutionary movement will be initiated through the ballot box with the aid of political opportunists who recognize the potential of the moment. Property, along with political power, will be increasingly centralized, and the freedom that can only be secured by broad property ownership will be lost. Only the plutocrats remain free.

Today the growth of the welfare state along with non-state concentrations of capital—BlackRock, Google, Amazon, etc.—provide for the steady concentration of both political and economic power. As capital is concentrated, as individuals are without property and eventually lose the taste for it, insecurity will invariably grow. And insecurity is the fuel of the welfare state, which opens the door to socialism. Today advocates of socialist policies capitalize on real and imagined insecurities to bring about a sweeping expansion of state power all in the name of equality, which is often mistaken for freedom.

No one understood this better than Tocqueville.

Tocqueville, the Genius of America, and a Warning

Seventeen years before Marx published the *Communist Manifesto* in 1848, Alexis de Tocqueville traveled to America. Although he was a scant twenty-five years old when he set sail, the result was his monumental book *Democracy in America*, published as two volumes (1835 and 1840). In this work Tocqueville sets out to understand the central features of American society. He argues that equality of conditions is the key to understanding American democracy. Whereas Europe, and especially France, was struggling with the effects of centuries of aristocratic rule, there was never an aristocracy in America. Equality of conditions existed

14. Marx, *The Marx-Engels Reader*, 490.

from the start. Tocqueville's book is an extended reflection on the differences between an aristocratic society and a democratic one, for it was
Tocqueville's conviction that the age of aristocracy was passing away and
an age of democracy was dawning.

While the topic of private property is not central to Tocqueville's
concerns, it does play a part. For instance, Tocqueville notes that in
aristocratic times, laws of primogeniture governed the transmission of
landed property and had the effect of keeping large estates intact for generations. With the abolition of primogeniture (a practice that was never
part of the law in America), landed property tended to be broken up as
fathers bequeathed equal shares to all their children.

Tocqueville notes that the battles over property and property rights
that were so common in Europe were unheard of in America. He attri-
butes this to the fact that Americans, as a whole, were property owners.
Tocqueville, no doubt reflecting on the recent revolution in his country,
notes that revolutions tend to threaten property; thus, in societies where
property is broadly owned, revolutionary fervor will be less likely to
arise. Tocqueville, in fact, ties democracy to property ownership. "Most
of those who inhabit democratic countries are property owners; they not
only have property, they live in the condition in which men attach the
most value to their property."[15] Widely distributed property, according
to Tocqueville, helps to cultivate a respect for the property of others, and
this general respect spills over to respect for the rights of others more
broadly. A propertied citizenry fosters political stability and is naturally
resistant to revolutionary temptations.

Tocqueville found in America a bustling commercial society, where
seemingly everyone was intent on pursuing material prosperity. He saw
that property ownership (or the possibility thereof) tends to stimulate
commercial activity, which tends in turn to increase the number of "eager
and anxious small proprietors."[16] The consequence was a steadily bur-
geoning middle class characterized by middle-class virtues and passions
that are directly traceable to property ownership. Tocqueville puts the
matter bluntly: "in America there are no proletarians."[17] In other words,
in America all were deeply vested in the culture of private property. It
becomes obvious in this light why socialism has taken so long to gain a

15. Tocqueville, *Democracy in America*, 608.

16. Tocqueville, Democracy in America, 608.

17. Tocqueville, *Democracy in America*, 228.

foothold in America, where the culture of private property was so deeply rooted. However, that culture has slowly eroded, and today we are witnessing the consequences of that erosion.

One of Tocqueville's goals is to understand the inner workings of a democratic society so that he can better see the likely road ahead. At the time he visited America, he was impressed by the decentralized nature of American economic activity. As he put it, "what strikes me most in the United States is not the extraordinary greatness of a few industrial enterprises, it is the innumerable multitude of small enterprises."[18] Small-scale businesses and family farms characterized the America Tocqueville saw, and he was convinced that this broad participation in economic activity, made possible by broadly distributed property, was a key factor in both the commercial energy and democratic success of America.

But as he attempts to imagine future developments, Tocqueville expresses concerns about possible changes in property as society shifts from an agricultural base to an industrial one. Tocqueville voices concerns similar to those Marx would make only a few years later. However, unlike Marx, who spoke in terms of a class struggle pitting the proletariat against the bourgeoisie, Tocqueville frames his analysis by highlighting the distinction between aristocracy and democracy. Tocqueville is convinced that democratic equality is the future and that aristocracy is dying, but he suggests a way that aristocracy could reemerge, and the impetus of this reversal would be large-scale industry replacing the multitude of small-scale enterprises.

Tocqueville notes that recent insights into economic theory and practice, most notably the division of labor and mass production, helped to increase production and decrease costs. While these changes may represent a boon for the consumer, Tocqueville is not as optimistic about the consequences for the worker. Like Marx, Tocqueville is convinced that certain work, wherein the worker spends his day performing a single simple task, will cause the worker to lose "the general faculty of applying his mind to the direction of his work." He becomes greatly skilled in a very precise task, but the finished product is beyond his view and soon beyond his concerns. Invoking the memorable image from Adam Smith's *The Wealth of Nations*, Tocqueville asks, "what should one expect from a man who has used twenty years of his life in making pinheads?"

18. Tocqueville, *Democracy in America*, 529.

Ultimately, "the man in him is degraded as the worker is perfected."[19] A society of perfect workers and degraded men is not one conducive to freedom.

Tocqueville was impressed by the creativity, initiative, and energy of the American people. He also noted that American culture was deeply formed by private property, and even those who did not possess property themselves were shaped by the aspiration to become property owners. But in a world characterized by the division of labor and mass production, Tocqueville foresaw a radical change. Rather than strong, independent citizens creatively seeking to improve their own property and therefore improve their lives, Tocqueville saw a situation in which "the worker becomes weaker, more limited, and more dependent."[20] At the same time as the worker slowly diminishes, those who possess capital will find ever new ways to profit from this new mode of production, for as production is concentrated, the possible profits are concentrated as well.

This new concentration of production and wealth will signal the rise of a new aristocracy. But unlike the older form of aristocracy, in which the nobles and peasants were tied to a particular piece of land and governed by reciprocal duties and responsibilities, this new industrial aristocracy will be different. "The manufacturer asks of the worker only his work, and the worker expects only a wage from him. The one is not engaged to protect, nor the other to defend, and they are not bound in a permanent manner either by habit or duty."[21] In this two-tiered society, the propertyless worker, who has become increasingly productive but simultaneously more limited in his capacities, works for a wage, and the industrialist reaps the benefits of this productivity. The worker "is in a continual, strict, and necessary dependence" on the "master." This, according to Tocqueville, is nothing other than industrial aristocracy. Tocqueville concludes his discussion with a warning: "The friends of democracy ought constantly to turn their regard with anxiety in this direction; for if ever permanent inequality of conditions and aristocracy are introduced anew into the world, one can predict that they will enter by this door."[22] Tocqueville is describing the rise of a new plutocratic class and a new class of propertyless workers.

19. Tocqueville, *Democracy in America*, 530.

20. Tocqueville, *Democracy in America*, 531.

21. Tocqueville, *Democracy in America*, 532.

22. Tocqueville, *Democracy in America*, 532.

This new industrial aristocracy would have been of great concern to many of America's founding generation. Indeed, the twentieth-century Swiss economist, Wilhelm Röpke, argues that Jefferson would have been appalled by the proletarianization of the American citizenry: "It was Jefferson's nightmare that the peasants and workers who comprised the population of the United States of America at the end of the eighteenth century would become changed one day into a propertyless and nomadic proletariat on the one hand and a capitalistic plutocracy on the other. This nightmare has come true within three generations."[23]

Rule by the wealthy is incompatible with democracy, which is rule by the people. A stable and healthy democracy is only possible in a society of property owners. To the extent that property is concentrated into fewer and fewer hands, and to the extent that a critical mass of citizens becomes propertyless nomadic proletarians, democracy itself becomes increasingly fragile, and eventually it will be only a charade. Of course, the plutocrats will have every incentive to encourage the illusion, to speak the language of democracy, to pay lip-service to democratic institutions and practices, but when property goes, so goes the possibility of independent, free citizens, the very kind of citizens necessary for a healthy and sustainable democratic society.

23. Röpke, *The Moral Foundations of Civil Society*, 138.

Chapter Five

Men at Work

Stewards in a Ragtag Garden

The basic aim of modern industrialism is not to make work
satisfying but to raise productivity; its proudest achievement
is labor saving, whereby labor is stamped with the mark of
undesirability.

—E.F. SCHUMACHER

IN A SHORT STORY titled "Quality," published in 1911, John Galsworthy
describes an old German boot-maker in London struggling to ply his
trade during the early years of the Industrial Revolution. The boot-maker,
Gessler is his name, considers himself an artist. He does exquisite work
using only the best materials. He trusts that people will pay for quality and that his reputation as a maker of superior boots will suffice to
keep his business thriving. However, mass-produced shoes, along with
relentless advertising, slowly but inexorably erode his business. Gessler's
boots are pricey, but they are also so well-constructed that they last for
years. Thus, even his regular customers don't come to his shop often. His
commitment to quality prevents him from cutting corners that would
make his wares less expensive and less durable. Only once, in a sudden
outburst, does he express anger and frustration: "dey get id by advertise-
ment, nod by work. Dey dake it away from us, who lofe our boods. Id

74

gomes to this—bresently I haf no work. Every year id gets less—you will see."[1]

Gessler's frustration is rooted in his love for his craft and his realization that his work is no longer appreciated. People want cheap boots without a wait, and because he makes each boot to fit a particular foot, his creations take time. Gessler's good work is replaced by the inferior products of machines pushed by advertisers more interested in making a profit than making boots.

Advertising and mass production have become even more prevalent in our day. Has the quality of our work suffered under the pressures of modern economic realities? Have economies of scale rendered quality less important and consumers apathetic? Has work itself changed in the process? Is there a connection between work and private property? To get at these questions, we need to inquire into the nature of work.

Is work a blessing or a curse? On the one hand, work can prove a deeply satisfying part of our lives, providing the avenue for fulfilling dreams, achieving goals, and making a difference in the world. On the other hand, work can be sheer drudgery. The day-in and day-out slogging through our respective responsibilities is often far from fulfilling. That most of us are compelled by circumstances to work casts a dark cloud over the entire enterprise and can leave us feeling trapped in an endless cycle of days laboring at tasks that are ultimately without meaning. Of course, we have all known people who claim to love their work, who hit the floor every day excited about the many satisfactions they claim to find at their jobs. Many others, however, "live lives of quiet desperation," as Thoreau so memorably put it. They play out their lives "working for the weekend," putting in their requisite forty hours as they plan for the respite that Saturday and Sunday provide and the all-too-short vacation in the summer. Many, while submitting to the daily grind, are buoyed by the dream of that glorious day when the Powerball numbers align and they can tell the boss to "take this job and shove it." At the very least, it's fair to say that we have a complicated relationship to work.

Work, of course, is a persistent part of the human condition. We read in the Creation account of Genesis that "the LORD God took the man, and put him into the garden of Eden to dress it and to keep it."[2]

1. Galsworthy, "Quality."
2. Genesis 2:15.

God appointed humans to cultivate the garden, to take the original Creation and intelligently tend it so that the goods latent in it could be fully realized. Stewardship is the operative notion here, for the prerogatives of ownership clearly belong to God, who created the garden in the first place. Exploitation, denigration, and wanton destruction of the garden would have been a violation of the trust that God delegated to the man. Stewardship is good work carried out with the long-term good of the object always in mind. Thus, even in paradise, one untouched by sin, decay, or email, there was work to do. If we are to take this story as somehow pointing to norms rooted in human existence itself, it appears that work is a natural part of human affairs and that a life without meaningful work is unfit for humans.

Of course, this isn't the whole story, for as we all know, the crafty serpent enticed the woman to eat the forbidden fruit, and the man willingly followed suit. Their eyes were opened, and they donned fig leaves to cover their nakedness. Because of their disobedience, God issued a series of curses. The serpent would forever crawl on its belly (one wonders what the uncursed serpent looked like), and the woman would experience pain in childbirth. God also changed the nature of work or at least the compliance of the natural world with human efforts: "cursed is the ground for thy sake; in sorrow shalt thou eat of it all the days of thy life; Thorns also and thistles shall it bring forth to thee; and thou shalt eat the herb of the field; In the sweat of thy face shalt thou eat bread, till thou return unto the ground."[3] As from the beginning, work is still our lot. And while many experience moments when work is reminiscent of the joyful stewardship of the unfallen world, most of us spend plenty of time sweating in the thistles and longing for a break.

The Fourth Commandment prohibits working on the Sabbath. The author points back to the Creation account to justify a weekly day of rest. "Remember the sabbath day, to keep it holy. Six days shalt thou labour, and do all thy work: But the seventh day is the sabbath of the LORD thy God: in it thou shalt not do any work....For in six days the LORD made heaven and earth, the sea, and all that in them is, and rested the seventh day: wherefore the LORD blessed the sabbath day, and hallowed it."[4] Even before the Fall, there existed a regular rhythm of work and rest. God Himself rested from His creative activity on the seventh day, and

3. Genesis 3:17.
4. Exodus 20:11.

according to the commandment we should likewise take a weekly break from our work.

The Sabbath is an example of a holy day when the mundane labors of which our lives generally consist give way to rest and, ultimately, to worship. It is described as belonging to the Lord; therefore, we are to imitate God's rest on the seventh day of Creation. Of course, a weekly Sabbath is not the only day that people set aside for rest. We all look forward to the various holidays that dot our calendars, and we are especially pleased when a holiday falls on a Friday or a Monday, thus bequeathing to us the coveted three-day weekend. We have even conjured up ways to make these special events occur more regularly by designating, for example, the first Monday in September as a holiday and by foisting the combined birthdays of Washington and Lincoln onto an innocent Monday in February. We have, in all of this, generally forgotten that "holiday" is a mash up of "holy day" and, aside from Christmas and Easter, we have done a pretty good job of keeping religion out of our holidays, which of course is an irony not to be ignored.

In our longing to escape from work, it is sometimes tempting to imagine a life consisting only of holidays (with pay). However, a holiday loses its meaning unless it is understood in the context of work. We can only anticipate and cherish a holiday if it is bookended by work days. Even more, holy days—that is, days set apart for God—make sense only in the context of "mundane days." This concept is, perhaps, better grasped when we consider that holy days are often thought of as days of feasting (the feasting, though not the worship, is carried over into many of our holidays). Easter, the greatest feast of the Christian calendar, for instance, comes at the conclusion of the forty-day Lenten fast. The feast makes sense in light of the fast that precedes it. If every day was a feast, the idea of a feast would be lost. If every day was a fast, our days would be unbearable. The fast prepares us for the feast even as the feast gives meaning to the fast. In short, the religious concept of a holy day suggests a proper rhythm for the week and for the entire year. These holy days can infuse our working days with meaning as they point us beyond the mundane to that which is sacred and therefore set apart.

Yet work itself is at best a mixture of satisfying effort and downright misery. This dual nature of work must be kept in mind, for if we think of work as wholly good and imagine that chafing against its demands is somehow a failure, then we are doomed to regular disappointment and frustration. However, if we think of work as a miserable necessity that we should escape whenever possible, we have forgotten that work is natural to humans and that perhaps a life of good work is the best sort of life, even better than a life of leisure, where the butler refills our glass as we lounge by the pool and someone less fortunate tends the garden.

A question remains, however: is some work better suited for humans than others? Or conversely, is some work degrading? Does some work elevate the worker while other work strips the worker of dignity? Or perhaps it is the work that is dignified or degraded by the person who engages it. If the former, then we need to give serious consideration to the kinds of work enjoined by our economic system. If the latter, then the work itself is not as much a concern as the kind of people we put to work: if we cultivate good character, good work will follow.

In our society so-called "knowledge workers" and other producers of non-tangible goods tend to be well paid and, unless they commit fraud or larceny, held in high esteem. (Whether they are held in high esteem because they are well-paid or vice-versa is an interesting question). On the other hand, manual laborers, that is, those who work with their hands, tend to be poorly paid and occupy an inferior social status. The farmer, trash-collector, and construction worker put in long hours, often in the blazing heat, soaking rain, or frigid winds. Their bodies are often uncomfortable, their hands are dirty, and physical exhaustion is simply part of the territory. For the rural worker, one who labors in the fields that produce the food that sustain us, words like "hick," "red-neck," and "bumpkin" point to the way these laborers are denigrated by those who consider themselves fortunate enough to keep their hands clean and their brows dry.

This division is, of course, nothing new. Aristotle, for instance, argued that there are three types of human lives. The first is a life dominated by the pursuit of pleasure. This is the life of the common man. For Aristotle, the vast majority of people engage in this sort of life. The second kind of life is one dedicated to the pursuit of honor. It is the political life in service to the state. Finally, and least common, is the life spent in pursuit of wisdom. This is the life given over to contemplation of the highest things. It is the life of the philosopher that, according to Aristotle, is the best life. This is the case because a life of contemplation is the most self-sufficient. On the other hand, a life dedicated to pursuing honor requires other people to confer the honor, and thus the public servant is not as self-sufficient as the philosopher. At the far extreme, the common man lives a life best suited to a cow, which is to say a slavish life in which immediate appetites govern behavior and serious thought is rare or non-existent.[5]

It's not difficult to see how Aristotle's categories set up a situation whereby physical work is seen as inferior to pure mental activity. The slave, the merchant, the farmer, and the craftsman all occupy a necessary but undesirable place in Aristotle's social hierarchy. The scholar stands at the top, a rare person whose mental gifts equip him for a life of study. Study is, of course, hard work. For Aristotle, it is the highest pursuit because it employs our rational capacity to contemplate eternal truths, the activity by which we most closely imitate God.

In this Aristotelian scheme, activities such as commerce, farming, building, or politics are necessary for a well-functioning city; however, there is a nearly audible sigh of relief from Aristotle that he doesn't have to engage in these inferior pursuits. Work, then, as Aristotle lays it out, is hierarchically ordered. And while many kinds of work are necessary, most work is degrading or engaged in only by inferior human beings incapable of philosophy.

St. Paul, a preacher who supported himself as a tent-maker, offers a vision of work noticeably different from Aristotle's. He bids his readers to "aspire to live quietly, and to mind your own affairs, and to work with your hands, as we instructed you."[6] In so doing, St. Paul inverts Aristotle's hierarchy: one should seek to work as a "vulgar craftsman" (Aristotle's term), using one's hands and not seek a public life of honor, much less commit oneself to a life of contemplation. Elsewhere he grants an equal status to any and all pursuits, emphasizing the heart of the worker rather than the kind of work: "Whatever you do, in word or deed, do everything in the name of the Lord Jesus, giving thanks to God the Father through him."[7] Of course, this does not imply that any kind of work whatsoever is now permissible. Prostitution, for instance, is impossible to engage "in the name of the Lord." Drug dealing and slave trading would not qualify. However, St. Paul undermines the Aristotelian hierarchy by, at the very least, making all legitimate professions equal and perhaps even privileging the manual arts.

Augustine reworks Aristotle's distinctions when he remarks that there are three kinds of life: one devoted to study, one devoted to activity,

5. Aristotle, *Nicomachean Ethics*, Book I, ch. 5; Book X, ch. 7–8.

6. I Thessalonians 4:11.

7. Colossians 3:17.

and a life comprised of a mixture of the two. He frames the discussion around Christ's teaching that the two greatest commandments are to love God and to love your neighbor.[8] For Augustine, a life devoted to study is a life dedicated to the pursuit of God. It is a life of contemplation and prayer. An active life is a life dedicated to serving one's neighbors. Thus, the kinds of life Augustine describes consist of a life dedicated to prayer, a life dedicated to service, and a life consisting of a mixture of both. Augustine argues that there is no one kind of life that is superior. Rather, a person might dedicate his life to prayer and study, but at the same time he should not neglect his neighbors. Alternatively, a person might pursue a life of service to others, but he should not neglect prayer. Thus, the ideal life for Augustine consists of a mixed life, though the exact ratios between prayer and service will differ from person to person. The Aristotelian life in pursuit of pleasure is, in Augustinian terms, simply not legitimate for the Christian.[9]

The term "vocation" has often been used by Christian thinkers to denote a call from God ("vocation" is derived from the Latin word meaning "to call"). It has often been employed especially to refer to a special call to the ministry. Today the word is generally used to refer to the manual arts, so that we see "vocational schools" where one "learns a vocation." This is both ironic and confused. It is ironic, for in the older sense, a vocation was a high and noble thing, and a person called into ministry was considered specially marked by God. Today people go to vocational school if they can't get into college or if they are not cut out for the abstract world of the knowledge industry. The word "vocation" has been stripped of any sense of calling and is reduced to a second-best choice made by those who can't successfully fill in the correct bubbles on the SAT or, more likely, who can't stand the thought of sitting behind a desk pushing papers forever.

 The German reformer, Martin Luther, made the concept of vocation a central piece of his theology. Luther chafed at the distinction between sacred and secular. He argued that all of life could be lived to the glory of God and that God works through vocation in the lives of every person, not only the lives of those called to serve the church. Thus, a person is called into a profession but so too a person is called to be a husband, a

---

8. Matthew 22:34–40.

9. Augustine, *City of God*, Book XIX, 19.

wife, a parent, a neighbor, a merchant, a builder, a nurse, or a friend. This expansive understanding of vocation recognizes the presence of God in all aspects of life. It therefore provides a concrete means by which a person can love God by loving his neighbor. Unlike the modern, deformed notion of vocation, Luther's account places God squarely in the center, for it is God who does the calling. When seen in this light, all work is dignified if God has called a person to it. If God calls you to be a minister, good. Do it to the glory of God. If He has called you to be a philosopher, good. If He has called you to be a businessman, a carpenter, a farmer, or a stay-at-home mom, good. The distinction between sacred and secular pursuits is removed, for if God calls you to a particular endeavor, surely it is holy.[10]

This expansive notion of vocation only makes sense in a world where God is actively involved in all aspects of life. With the decline of Christianity and a corresponding decline in belief in a personal God, we shouldn't be surprised that the idea of vocation changed. Instead of seeking the call of God, we now ask young people what they want to do with their lives. Providence and divine guidance oriented toward service to others has been replaced with individual will rooted in appetite. Because appetites are infinitely expansive as well as notoriously fickle, it is no surprise that the language of self-fulfillment has largely usurped that of service. The result is that now a primary consideration for one's vocation (in the modern sense) is monetary. After all, if I choose my job in order to satisfy my desires, I would do well to select a job that pays well so that my desires can be more readily sated.

Tocqueville argues that in ages of equality, where aristocracies have disappeared along with inherited wealth, "the idea of work as a necessary, natural, and honest condition of humanity is therefore offered to the human mind on every side." The result? Work is honored. Tocqueville noted that rich Americans found it necessary to travel to Europe if they wanted to idle away their days without work. Such a leisurely life was more acceptable in Europe, where some vestiges of an aristocracy still remained. Furthermore, in aristocracies "it is not precisely work that is scorned, but work with a view to profit. Work is glorious when ambition or virtue alone makes one undertake it."[11] Thus, the aristocrat scorns the life of the laborer, farmer, or craftsman who works for money but admires

10. For a helpful exploration of Luther on vocation see Veith, *God at Work*.

11. Tocqueville, *Democracy in America*, 525.

a life given to the pursuit of honor. Here we see two of Aristotle's lives represented, but the third, the life of philosophy, has faded into obscurity.

Tocqueville was impressed by the active energy that pervaded the American society. But this activity was restless and impatient. Thus, Tocqueville thought that agriculture—an endeavor that, for all its charms, is no way to quick riches—would be eclipsed by commerce, which promises the possibility of faster returns. Tocqueville was convinced that agriculture, itself, would become more industrialized as impatient Americans sought to make it generate immediate profits. Of course, he didn't foresee the remarkable way these industrial farmers would avail themselves of government subsidies, thus providing guaranteed profits in a notoriously fickle endeavor.

This urge to get rich quickly would, Tocqueville worried, shape the American character so that the idea of chance would become a sort of intoxicating drug. This love of risk would shape the way commerce, and life in general, developed. Gambling, lotteries, speculation, and more recently the futures markets, options trading, and credit default swaps all have one thing in common: they are characterized by risk that holds out the tantalizing possibility of huge profits with little or no work. In a society where profits made in these activities are seen as the ideal way to get rich, practices like saving for the future, thrift, and responsibility will be exchanged for the ephemeral belief that a jackpot is just around the corner if I can only muster one more quarter for the lucky machine. It is little wonder that in such a society public and private debt would skyrocket beyond imagination, for a society of optimistic gamblers will be animated by the belief that either a fix is coming or that the party will keep on rolling until we are safely dead. In this way, the nobility of work is undermined and replaced with the notion that work is the necessary evil that our games of chance will one day render unnecessary—freedom from work is the ideal toward which many now strive or at least aspire.

As we have seen, while Tocqueville was considering the social and political consequences of democracy, Marx was mulling over the social and political nature of labor in a capitalist system. He was convinced that in a capitalist society the nature of work is fundamentally different from work in a pre-capitalist society or in a future communist society. Echoing the concerns of the Luddites, he found that the division of labor along with machine technology all too often reduced the worker to merely "an appendage of the machine."[12] Such a worker finds himself alienated from the product of his labor. He no longer has the satisfaction of seeing a piece of work through from start to finish; therefore, he no longer has the opportunity to affix his name proudly to the finished product. The worker becomes alienated from his work, so that "he is at home when he is not working, and when he is working he is not at home."[13] Today it is not only factory workers who find themselves alienated from any definitive product. Middle managers and government bureaucrats are often similarly bereft of any concrete, tangible product associated with their work.

Marx, here, was merely echoing a sentiment expressed by Adam Smith. While most know Smith for his celebration of the division of labor (and its resulting pins), Smith recognizes a darker side of the story. According to Smith, a person who performs the same simple task "has no occasion to exert his understanding" and as a consequence "becomes as stupid and ignorant as it is possible for a human creature to become." Such a person becomes incapable of "rational conversation" and is barely able to make decisions for his own life, let alone grasp the "interests of his country" and thereby qualify himself to participate in the government. Ultimately, "his dexterity at his own particular trade seems, in this manner, to be acquired at the expense of his intellectual, social, and martial virtues." Smith insists this is the necessary condition of the working class in "every improved and civilized society," and the "great body of the people" will find themselves debased "unless government takes some pains to prevent it."[14] This is a real concern if we recall Webster's insistence that a free society requires citizens who are broadly educated owners of property. It is also worth noting that the father of modern capitalism believes there is a role for government to prevent and correct problems caused by market forces.

In his book *Ideas Have Consequences*, Richard Weaver argues that specialization fragments individuals, competencies, and societies. This fragmentation, at the level of individuals, produces a character that is not compatible with wisdom and is therefore not capable of self-government, much less the government of others. As he puts it, "specialization develops only part of a man; a man partially developed is deformed; and one

12. Marx, *The Marx-Engels Reader*, 479.
13. Marx, *The Marx-Engels Reader*, 74.
14. Adam Smith, *Wealth of Nations*, vol. 2, pg. 781–2.

deformed is the last person to be thought of as a ruler."[15] This sort of deformation by specialization is clearly exemplified, according to Weaver, in the Manhattan Project. Thousands were employed in the undertaking, yet to maintain secrecy each person was compelled to focus exclusively on his specialized task without knowledge of the end toward which everyone was working. But, Weaver asks, should not the end of a project be of concern to all involved? The result of this isolation by specialization is that each individual, unaware of and unconcerned with the ends to which his labors are directed, becomes, in Weaver's words, "ethical eunuchs."[16] People of this sort are competent in one specific task or field. They are completely focused on mediate ends and the means by which to achieve those ends. The final end remains beyond the purview of their concern, and as a result their perceived responsibility ends at the frontiers of their respective specialties. However, wisdom, and with it good judgment, requires some understanding of the whole, and an understanding of the whole is less likely when the functions of workers are so fragmented and narrow that all they see is a tiny part of the process.

Such a criticism suggests that the solution to the problem is to be found in abandoning the division of labor and returning to a pre-industrial model of independent craftsmen where a single, skilled individual produces an item from start to finish. Clearly there are serious limitations to this "solution." Some division of labor and specialization is necessary for any developed economy. However, it is worth asking whether the division of labor can be tempered so that the benefits can be realized while the liabilities can be limited. Economist E.F. Schumacher writes of "human scale technologies" that avoid the drawbacks of colossal industrial enterprises while at the same time making modern technology available.[17] An added advantage of these smaller scale technologies is that they require less capital, and therefore individuals, small communities, and even developing countries can reap the benefits. Of course, such technologies may not be universally practical, but too little consideration is given to human scale in our economic arrangements. Thinking more explicitly in terms of human scale will likely open up new possibilities where none were previously seen or imagined.

15. Weaver, *Ideas Have Consequences*, 56.

16. Weaver, *Ideas Have Consequences*, 65.

17. Schumacher, *Small is Beautiful*, chapter 5.

In terms of organization, worker-owned companies keep the workers directly involved in the management of the company even if the various jobs are discrete and, as Marx put it, alienating. Indeed, from the perspective of his work, the worker-owner may be alienated from the finished product, but as an owner/manager he is necessarily engaged in running the organization and therefore is reunited to the end product. Both human-scaled technology and worker-owned endeavors suggest ways that work can be revitalized in a world where the division of labor is a reality.

Of course, technology that requires comparatively little capital as well as worker-owned enterprises both suggest that property lies at the heart of our investigation into work. It may be that workers whose work is directed towards their own property are significantly different from proletarian workers who labor only for a wage. Marx looked forward to the day when the proletariat would rise up against the propertied class. But if Marx saw the proletarianization of the worker as the necessary precursor to the revolution, others have emphasized the corrupting effects of proletarianized democracy. According to Wilhelm Röpke, in a world of propertyless wage-earners the nature of work itself changes.

> Work instead of being a satisfaction and fulfillment of life becomes a mere means and the hours spent at work a mere liability, whereas normally these ought to represent an asset in the balance-sheet of life. Compensation for this state of affairs is sought all the more eagerly in consumption, but more often than not this means compensation in pleasures and distractions which are no less mechanical and void than the work. This floating humanity, the modern nomads as may well be understood— feel an intense longing for something which must be lacking to a great extent in such an existence, i.e., security and stability.[18]

The proletarian thinks primarily in terms of wages. Wages have an *exchange value*, but apart from exchange, they are inert. On the other hand, real, tangible property has both a *use value* as well as an exchange value. A table, a bicycle, or an electric mixer can all be sold in the marketplace. But additionally, their value can be realized apart from exchange. They can be put to practical use in a way that a dollar bill cannot. Some kinds of property also have *production value*. I can work my land and produce food for myself and my family; with my tools I can build a chair

---

18. Röpke, *The Moral Foundations of a Free Society*, 140.

to rest in or a house to live in; I can also create marketable items and sell them for profit or trade them for goods I need or desire. Property characterized by production value is a form of property best suited to independence, for it provides the owner with broader effective control than property suited merely to exchange or to use. In times of economic difficulty, the ownership of productive land, even a garden plot in a suburb or on a rooftop in the city, provides produce both for sustenance and for exchange. The proletarian is bereft of productive property and therefore his options are constricted, for all his decisions must be made in terms of exchange. He lacks effective control over a piece of property, and as a result the scope of his freedom is narrower than the freedom of the owner of productive property.

The production value of property can take a passive or active form. Passive production comes in the form of accrued interest. Acquiring capital that can be put to work in passive production generally requires active production, which generally consists of serious and sustained work. Running a farm or a business, growing a garden, or operating the tools of a trade all require skills that take time and experience to acquire. They require commitment to learning a craft and, in many instances, they require long term commitment to a particular place. One's mobility is severely reduced when cultivating a piece of land is the goal. The same sort of stability is required for many businesses. Intelligent attention and care must be paid to the land if it is to yield a consistent harvest. Attention to the needs of one's customers is required for a business to thrive.

According to Röpke, an economy consisting primarily of wage laborers is one that fosters both insecurity and instability. Wage laborers often find themselves living paycheck-to-paycheck out of necessity when wages are low, or out of habit when surplus wages are seen as a means to indulge the appetites. Living close to the margin, whether by necessity or by carelessness, fosters insecurity. When the threat of unemployment looms during times of local or national crisis, the insecurity becomes acute. Workers who are unattached to a piece of land or to the infrastructure of a small business or workshop will be easily induced to relocate in a relentless search for wages and some semblance of security. Here we see the surge of the nomadic proletarian, the sort of unattached worker championed by many libertarians.[19]

---

19. For example, in his book critiquing socialism, the economist Ludwig von Mises asserts that if workers "did not act as trade unionists, but reduced their demands and changed their locations and occupations according to the requirements of the labour

When security and stability are undermined, and when the independence afforded by the ownership of productive property is lost, the stage is set for the emergence of the welfare state. Röpke is unambiguous on this point: "Government-organized relief for the masses is simply the crutch of a society crippled by proletarianism, an expedient adapted to the economic and moral immaturity of the classes which emerged from the decomposition of the old social order." According to Röpke, the welfare state can only be dispensed with "in the degree in which we may hope to overcome that inglorious period of proletarianization and rootlessness."[20] In other words, the decline of private property and the independence that such property affords creates proletarian citizens lacking in both security and stability. Such citizens, and their elected officials, are champions of the welfare state, for government programs hold out the promise of both security and stability. The proletarians demand it, and their representatives give them what they demand, for in a democratic system the people call the tune and their representatives dance the dance. The growth of the welfare system facilitates the steady growth of the state, for there is little incentive short of economic ruin (and sometimes that is even inadequate) to curtail its growth.

Röpke's description of the welfare state as the product of the "economic and moral immaturity" of its citizens is startling in its bluntness. He is suggesting that the ownership of property serves to create citizens who are adults, both economically and morally. Economically, property teaches self-sufficiency and fosters a spirit of independence that makes the property-owner better equipped to help his distressed neighbor and in so doing create an alternative to the welfare state. Morally, property ownership encourages the cultivation of virtues like self-control, thrift, personal responsibility, neighborliness, and grit. When a society is comprised of citizens with these virtues, a large welfare apparatus is not necessary. Furthermore, many citizens possessing such virtues would be loath to accept government payments even if they were available.

On the other hand, a society of economically and morally immature citizens is a society of children. If citizens lack economic self-sufficiency and instead look to the state to meet their basic needs, they are exhibiting the behavior of children—orphans bereft of any support system. In moral terms, if citizens lack the virtues of self-control, spend

---

market, they could eventually find work." Mises, *Socialism*, 485.

    20. Röpke, *A Humane Economy*, 154.

like profligates, and shun personal responsibility, they are behaving like spoiled children. Children, of course, need a parent to provide for them, and spoiled children need the firm hand of a master. Unfortunately, the aptly named "nanny state" is all-too willing to play the role of the parent, eagerly, although often clumsily, meeting the economic and social needs of its dependents. However, the firm hand of a master, the very thing most needed by a spoiled child, is less likely, especially in a democracy, for in a democracy those who are dolling out the goodies depend on their constituents for their power. Thus, the discipline that a spoiled child so desperately needs is not forthcoming, and the welfare state lumbers along, encouraging the very pathologies that nourish it and facilitate its growth.

A welfare state populated by economically and morally immature citizens is a fragile thing. Spoiled children have their incessant demands, and when their demands are not met they are quite willing to throw tantrums. Immature democratic citizens throw tantrums at the ballot box, and they organize protests demanding government action, which invariably takes the form of handouts. Ultimately, a welfare society undermines the culture of private property and in so doing undermines the vital work ethic that well-secured property ownership fosters. A decrease in property ownership and a decline in the appreciation for work, combined with an expanding welfare state, increases personal insecurity and social instability and necessitates the expansion of the police powers of the state. It is for this reason that a growing welfare state is historically accompanied by a growing police state. Needless to say, a growing police state combined with insecure and anxious citizens is a situation ripe for the abuse of power, and when police powers are abused, law-enforcement itself can easily be scapegoated by the spoiled children of the revolution. The 'defund the police' movement will, where it is implemented, lead to surges in crime, greater insecurity, and ultimately further strengthen state power.

We are presented here with two alternatives, both offering strikingly different social and political visions. On the one hand, a culture of work, undergirded by a vibrant culture of private property, gives rise to a spirit of independence, self-sufficiency, self-control, and personal responsibility. These are the very qualities necessary for citizens of a free society. A spirit of neighborliness characterizes such citizens, and those with real needs are helped financially but also in ways that go beyond economics. On the other hand, a culture of social services calls forth a spirit of dependence. The generous and creative spirit of neighborliness is replaced by the cold bureaucratic functionary whose responsibility to distribute aid to the poor lacks the creative and personal element that neighborliness affords. The erosion of private property and a corresponding erosion of the culture of work create a condition that is conducive to servitude. The loss of a culture of work, economic and moral immaturity, insecurity, and the rise of the police state create a toxic mix where freedom is replaced by state power. If freedom is an ideal worth cherishing, a society characterized by property and good work is an indispensable ingredient. It is the vocation of free citizens to create such a society.

Chapter Six

Plutocrats, Socialists,
and American Politics

But private property ought to be protected against much bigger
things than burglars and pickpockets. It needs protection
against the plots of a whole plutocracy.

—G.K. CHESTERTON

IN A 2015 CAMPAIGN ad Bernie Sanders announced that he was "taking
on Wall Street and a corrupt political system that keeps in place a rigged
system."[1] In a speech during the same campaign season, he declared
that "Wall Street, corporate America, the corporate media, and wealthy
campaign donors are just too powerful."[2]

In a 2016 opinion piece published by *The Washington Post*, billionaire political influencer Charles Koch declared that, despite their
significant differences, he agreed with Bernie Sanders on an important
point. And though neither use the term, both are describing a plutocratic
system that both agree is fundamentally unjust. Here's Koch:

> The senator is upset with a political and economic system that
> is often rigged to help the privileged few at the expense of ev-
> eryone else, particularly the least advantaged. He believes that
> we have a two-tiered society that increasingly dooms millions

1. Frizell, *Time*, June 16, 2016.
2. Sanders, *Market Watch*, Jan. 5, 2016.

of our fellow citizens to lives of poverty and hopelessness. He
thinks many corporations seek and benefit from corporate welfare while ordinary citizens are denied opportunities and a level
playing field.

I agree with him.

Democrats and Republicans have too often favored policies
and regulations that pick winners and losers. This helps perpetuate a cycle of control, dependency, cronyism and poverty in the
United States. These are complicated issues, but it's not enough
to say that government alone is to blame. Large portions of the
business community have actively pushed for these policies.

Of course, Koch did not endorse Sanders. While they agreed on
the diagnosis, the two men diverged dramatically over policy prescrip-
tions: Sanders advocated increased government involvement to rectify
inequalities and foster a stronger and healthier middle class. Koch, on the
other hand, wanted the government to attend to only a few very limited
matters and in the process let the free market allocate resources and rewards according to the logic of the invisible hand. However, the government has so distorted the market that it is far from the libertarian ideal
championed by Koch. Here's Koch again:

> Consider the regulations, handouts, mandates, subsidies and
> other forms of largesse our elected officials dole out to the
> wealthy and well-connected. The tax code alone contains $1.5
> trillion in exemptions and special-interest carve-outs. Anti-
> competitive regulations cost businesses an additional $1.9 tril-
> lion every year. Perversely, this regulatory burden falls hardest
> on small companies, innovators and the poor, while benefitting
> many large companies like ours. This unfairly benefits estab-
> lished firms and penalizes new entrants, contributing to a two-
> tiered society.[3]

Sanders gave voice in the 2016 election cycle to a sentiment that
had been building for some time. Back in 2004 North Carolina Senator John Edwards, while running for president, spoke of the increasing
income disparity that was creating "Two Americas." Edwards lost in the
primaries but was tapped by John Kerry to serve as his running mate. At
the 2004 Democratic Convention Edwards reprised his Two Americas
theme:

---

3. Koch, *The Washington Post*, Feb. 18, 2016

The truth is, we still live in a country where there are two different Americas . . . [applause] one, for all of those people who have
lived the American dream and don't have to worry, and another
for most Americans, everybody else who struggle to make ends
meet every single day. It doesn't have to be that way. . . . So let me
give you some specifics. First, we can create good-paying jobs in
this country again. We're going to get rid of tax cuts for companies who are outsourcing your jobs . . . [applause] and, instead,
we're going to give tax breaks to American companies that are
keeping jobs right here in America. . . . Well, let me tell you how
we're going to pay for it. And I want to be very clear about this.
We are going to keep and protect the tax cuts for 98 percent of
Americans—98 percent. We're going to roll back—going to roll
back the tax cuts for the wealthiest Americans. And we're going
to close corporate loopholes.[4]

With the 2008–9 economic collapse and subsequent Wall Street
bailout, it became clear that some individuals and companies were not
treated like the rest of us. "Too Big to Fail" emerged as a phrase indicat-
ing that, if a corporation became big enough, its poor financial decisions
would be insured by the federal government. Thus, in practical terms,
losses were absorbed by the public and profits were enjoyed privately.
This, of course, created a powerful incentive to take risks, since the private rewards were potentially massive while the losses were offloaded
onto the public.

In the fall of 2011, in response to an ad in the anti-consumerist
magazine *Adbusters*, protesters converged in lower Manhattan near
the charging bull statue on Wall Street. The protesters eventually made
their way to Zuccotto Park, a small private park nearby. For the next two
months this band of disparate but generally disgruntled individuals—
some professionals by day and protesters by night, some just professional
protesters—attempted to make their voices heard and at the same time to
live in a cobbled together tent community. Their concerns were varied,
but in general terms this Occupy Wall Street Movement, as it came to be
called, objected to wealth inequality and the excessive influence of corporations, and they championed economic justice as a means of promoting
social justice.

The protest was mostly peaceful, and at least initially New York
City Mayor Michael Bloomberg was supportive: "People have a right to

---

4. Edwards, *CBS News*, July 28, 2004.

protest, and if they want to protest, we'll be happy to make sure they have locations to do it."[5] When police threatened to arrest protesters for using a bullhorn, the protesters adopted the "human microphone" technique whereby one person would speak and the crowd would repeat what the speaker just said in a sort of call and response cadence that would, they hoped, be more effective and louder than a microphone. The technique would also foster solidarity, as passive listening was changed to active engagement through repetition. The protesters marched through the financial district chanting such slogans as "We are the 99 percent" and "This is what democracy looks like."

In November, however, the mayor decided that a long-term tent city in downtown Manhattan was not in the best interests of public safety, good order, or good hygiene. In an early morning raid, riot police cleared the area. Some present accused the police of using excessive force, but the media was barred from the area, so accounts are sketchy. Nevertheless, it was clear that Bloomberg had soured on the Occupy crowd. Following the raid, his office released a statement: "No right is absolute and with every right comes responsibilities.... The First Amendment protects speech—it does not protect the use of tents and sleeping bags to take over a public space."[6]

Although the tents only stood for two short months in the fall of 2011, the Occupy Wall Street movement, despite its lack of overall focus, helped to illuminate a set of concerns that resonated with many, even with some who did not ordinarily sympathize with the broader concerns of the left or the general tactics of protest.

In September of 2011, as Occupy Wall Street was at its height, Harvard law professor Elizabeth Warren declared her intent to run for the U.S. Senate. As an attorney and professor, she specialized in bankruptcy and commercial law, which provided an ideal background for her to address the concerns of the Occupy movement. In September of the next year, while in the final leg of her Senatorial race, Warren was tapped to deliver a prime-time speech at the Democratic National Convention, a speech that propelled her to national prominence and positioned her as a rising star on the progressive wing of the Democratic Party. Like Sanders, Warren claimed the system was "rigged" in favor of the wealthy and powerful, and that the middle class had been left with nothing other than

5. Earle, "A Brief History of Occupy," pg. 3.
6. Earle, "A Brief History of Occupy," pg. 9.

a suspicion that something was amiss. "Here's the painful part: they're right. The system is rigged. Billionaires pay lower taxes than their secretaries." She continued with an attack on Wall Street, personified in the Republican candidate and successful venture capitalist, Mitt Romney. "Republicans say they don't believe in government. Sure they do. They believe in government to help themselves and their powerful friends. Mitt Romney's the guy who said corporations are people. No, Governor Romney, corporations are not people. People have hearts, they have kids. . . . They live, they love, and they die. And that matters."[7] Warren won the Senate seat handily.

In 2019 Warren declared her intention to run for the White House. In June, her campaign published "A Plan for Economic Patriotism." The title itself suggests a populist sentiment that diverged from the globalist views that seem to animate the most radical of the Woke Socialists. In this document Warren expressed her appreciation for the opportunities she enjoyed as an American but lamented the fact that many "American" corporations have little loyalty to America. Instead, they have relocated their manufacturing to nations with lower labor costs, lower tax rates, and fewer regulations, in the process "abandoning loyal American workers and hollowing out American cities." She blamed politicians as well as corporate leaders:

> Politicians love to say they care about American jobs. But for decades, those same politicians have cited "free market principles" and refused to intervene in markets on behalf of American workers. And of course, they ignore those same supposed principles and intervene regularly to protect the interests of multinational corporations and international capital. The result? Millions of good jobs lost overseas and a generation of stagnant wages, growing inequality, and sluggish economic growth.

Warren proposed an agenda of "economic patriotism, using new and existing tools to defend and create quality American jobs and promote American industry" with the goal of "putting American workers and middle-class prosperity [not property] ahead of multinational profits and Wall Street bonuses."[8]

Perhaps surprisingly, Warren's economic plan had much in common with the economic nationalism of Donald Trump. One pundit

7. Kirchgaessner, *Financial Times*, Sept. 6, 2012.
8. Warren, "A Plan for Economic Patriotism," June 4, 2019.

remarked that Warren's plan "sounds like Donald Trump at his best."[9] At the same time Warren called herself a progressive, and many of her social policy proposals were difficult to distinguish from politicians who call themselves socialists. Like Sanders, Warren supported free college tuition and the elimination of student debt.[10] Like Sanders, Warren supported replacing private health insurance with a publicly funded single-payer system. She also came out in support of the Green New Deal.[11]

Bernie Sanders met with significant success in both the 2016 the 2020 primaries. Unlike the other major Democratic candidates, he did not shy away from calling himself a socialist. Of course, he was careful to identify himself as a "democratic socialist" and not simply a socialist. According to The Democratic Socialists of America website, "Democratic socialists believe that both the economy and society should be run democratically—to meet public needs, not to make profits for a few. To achieve a more just society, many structures of our government and economy must be radically transformed through greater economic and social democracy so that ordinary Americans can participate in the many decisions that affect our lives." Furthermore, "Democracy and socialism go hand in hand. All over the world, wherever the idea of democracy has taken root, the vision of socialism has taken root as well—everywhere but in the United States. Because of this, many false ideas about socialism have developed in the US." Democratic socialists do not, they insist, advocate for an "all-powerful government bureaucracy," but at the same time they do not want "big corporate bureaucracies" to exist either. Instead, "we believe that the workers and consumers who are affected by economic institutions should own and control them." In practical terms, "social ownership could take many forms, such as worker-owned cooperatives or publicly owned enterprises managed by workers and consumer representatives. Democratic socialists favor as much decentralization as possible."[12]

Of course, that final sentence is crucial. How much decentralization is possible given the economic and social outcomes the socialists champion? While they may employ the language of decentralization, in practical terms socialists in American today seem committed to dramatic

9. Wu, *USA Today*, June 6, 2019.

10. Hess, *CNBC*, April 23, 2019.

11. Khalid, *Daily Dot*, April 22, 2019.

12. *Democratic Socialists of America*. Website.

increases in government spending and power with little concern that the social programs they support would be purchased—or more accurately stolen via deficit spending—from future citizens who have no voice in the matter. That, at the very least, is a constricted notion of both democracy and social justice, a view that future generations will no doubt find unacceptable or downright immoral. Of course, main-stream Republicans seem just as willing as the socialists to indulge in the spending spree. Thus, while their political rhetoric and ostensible goals may differ, both sides seem quite willing to ignore any fiscal or moral responsibility to future generations.

In the wake of the 2018 mid-term elections there was a decided shift in the tone and tactics employed by those advocating change, especially those on the far left who embraced the new religion of wokeness. This radical wing virtually took over the Democratic Party, and moderates were left with the difficult choice of adopting the posture and policies of the radicals or being left behind. With the perception that the only alternative to the Left was the Trump-dominated Republican Party, it's not surprising that many moderate Democrats read the tea leaves and embraced, or at least acquiesced to, the new Woke Socialism.

One feature of this shift was an increasing tendency (though not entirely new) to forgo debate in favor of protest. Debate implies deliberation and is only possible when both sides assume the other is arguing in good faith and that a rational solution—often rooted in compromise—can be found. The politics of protest, on the other hand, implicitly denies the effectiveness of rational discussion and instead attempts to leverage power in service of the ideals championed by the protestor. Rather than assuming that both sides are acting in good faith, the politics of protest is animated by the assumption that one's opponent is acting with evil intent. Compromise is only tactical, and one will never compromise if ultimate victory—ideally the destruction of one's opponent—is possible. There is little doubt that the tactics of many on the Woke Left are primarily rooted in the logic—or illogic—of protest. The same emotion-laden convulsions characterized some pro-Trump protesters on the Right in the aftermath of the 2020 presidential election.

This is not to say that all protest is illegitimate or that the tactics of protest only emerged with Occupy Wall Street or the Civil Rights Movement of the 1960s. Indeed, one of the most famous incidents of the American Founding era was a protest. On December 16, 1773 a group of colonists badly disguised as Mohawk Indians boarded ships loaded with tea that were anchored in Boston Harbor. The tea was owned by the East India Company, a company that was in financial trouble but had been deemed too big to fail by the British government. In an attempt to save the company, Parliament gave it a monopoly on the tea trade in the American colonies and at the same time exempted the company from certain export taxes, thereby subsidizing the product, even undercutting the prices of smuggled tea. Hidden in the subsidy was a small tax that was intended to make a point: despite the protestations of certain radicals among the colonists, Parliament could in fact levy taxes on the colonies even though the colonies were not represented in Parliament. The colonists saw through the ruse and steeped the tea in the harbor. Tensions continued to escalate until that fateful day in April 1775 when a shot heard round the world signaled the beginning of the American War for Independence.

The Woke Socialists insist that we are at another moment of crisis in our nation's history. Economic inequalities have become so acute, power disparities have become so pronounced, and the climate crisis has reached such a point that a new revolution is needed. Indeed, in 2019 Congresswoman Alexandria Ocasio-Cortez established an online clock counting down to a climate-induced apocalypse. The website announces that "climate change and our environmental challenges are one of the biggest existential threats to our way of life, not just as a nation, but as a world."[13] The countdown puts the end of the world on January 21, 2031. We have, in other words, only a short window of time to act aggressively, radically, and decisively to save the world, ourselves, and our children from disaster. For all the talk of decentralization from the Democratic Socialists, AOC's call to action does not take that path. The language of crisis is perhaps the most effective means by which power is consolidated into the hands of a demagogue who promises salvation. Bernie Sanders and Elizabeth Warren want to break up the banks and break up Google and Facebook, and they are right to see that concentrations of economic power—especially when that power has colluded with the state—is dangerous. But they go on to insist on universal health care (even for illegal aliens), free college tuition, and a universal income all while kowtowing to demands to arrest climate change and implement the woke social agenda. Decentralization of political power is lost in this orgy of pandering to voters, many of whom seem primarily interested in

13. AOC Countdown Clock.

getting free stuff and making the wealthy foot the bill. The coronavirus only added to the sense of urgency. A public health crisis combined with an economic crisis and overlaid by a looming climate apocalypse seemed to justify an unprecedented expansion of government "generosity" and "attention." The protests and chaos following the death of George Floyd revealed a strange mix of antinomianism and infantilism. Protesters who seemed quite happy to destroy the property of others demanded the defunding of the police and an increase of funds for services.[14] The cipher candidate Joe Biden was pulled from a death spiral in the primaries and, with the backing of Big Media and Big Tech, won the White House and dutifully set about repaying his political debts. In the process political and economic power continued to merge, and the plutocracy continued to solidify its position.

Of course, concerns about cronyism, businesses that are too big to fail, and state-aided monopolies are not unique to any one group. On this point, as we have seen, Charles Koch and Bernie Sanders find common ground. Others in the past have noted the same constellation of problems.

In his neglected classic, *The Servile State* (1912), Hilaire Belloc argued that capitalism is fundamentally unstable and is therefore a transitory condition. It is important, though, to pay careful attention to his definition of capitalism. "A society in which the ownership of the means of production is confined to a body of free citizens not large enough to make up properly a general character of that society, while the rest are dispossessed of the means of production and therefore proletarian, we call capitalist."[15] For Belloc capitalism is synonymous with plutocracy, and there are only two resolutions to the inherent instability. The first is socialism and the second is what he calls "the distributist state" or "the proprietary state" in which private property, specifically the means of production, is broadly distributed throughout the populace.

Capitalism as Belloc defines it tends toward centralization of economic power, but when economic power is centralized it requires a strong political structure to manage it. Again, we see a connection that is too often ignored: centralized economic power goes hand-in-hand with centralized political power. Belloc's friend G.K. Chesterton argued that capitalism had come to an end, and the evidence was that the capitalists

14. Levin, *The Guardian*, June 4, 2020.
15. Belloc, *The Servile State*, 107.

appealed "for the intervention of Government like Socialists."[16] In light of the cry for a government bailout in 2008–9, and the enthusiasm for increased government power to address the climate crisis and coronavirus, it is difficult not to see Chesterton's point.

The classical liberal economist F.A. Hayek argued that consolidation of economic power in the form of monopolies will invariably lead toward socialism. "A state which allows such enormous aggregations of power [Amazon? Google? Facebook?] to grow up cannot afford to let this power rest entirely in private control." The blame, according to Hayek, does not fall exclusively upon the capitalist class. Instead, "the fatal development was that they have succeeded in enlisting the support of an ever-increasing number of other groups and, with their help, obtaining the support of the state."[17] In other words, the centralization of economic power leads to the centralization of state power. Today some socialists at least feign concern about concentrations of non-state power. However, they are completely oblivious to the dangers of the power of the state that their policies will necessarily call forth.

It is important to note that both plutocrats and socialists tend to speak in terms of wealth rather than property. This is a significant change from the Founding Era when leaders, as we have seen, insisted that property and freedom are inseparable. This shift from property to wealth mirrors changes in our conception of freedom and can help us better grasp our current maladies. We can identify the main contours of this change over the course of American history.

From the American colonial era into the early twentieth century, property was primarily conceived in physical terms and was exemplified in land, but would also include a business or the tools of one's trade. Property in its truest form was productive. It could produce wealth and therefore it could sustain a family. A person who owned productive property—capital, as the economists put it—was independent to the degree that he could provide for himelf and his family. This independence gave birth to a political freedom that was unmistakable, though limited by the realities of daily existence. Property generally demanded effort, so the need to work and the reality of freedom were inseparable. And this independence was not the rugged independence romantically envisioned by some on the Right. Independence was more properly conceived as

16. Chesterton, *The Outline of Sanity*, 42.
17. Hayek, *The Road to Serfdom*, 214, 215.

interdependence whereby neighbors could aid and support each other by means of the productive property they possessed. The broad ownership of real property provided the material conditions for a vigorous conception of freedom and simultaneously kept at bay the expansion of state power, for nothing more effectively calls forth state power than proletarian masses plagued by insecurity and in desperate need of basic goods. Of course, political freedom was not always extended as broadly as it could, and should, have been. Nevertheless, the potential was there, and the ideal was exemplified by the promise, sadly not carried out, that former slaves would receive "forty acres and a mule."[18] It was understood that the freedom of former slaves consisted not simply in a declaration of emancipation or the abolition of slavery. Instead, effective freedom was seen as tied inextricably to economic independence characterized by the ownership of capital. The ideal, expressed here in terms of land and livestock, was that a family—understood as the most basic economic unit—was most truly free if it possessed the means of production required to support itself. The ideal form of property was real, durable, and productive. Freedom was inseparable from the responsibility and work that made a family self-sufficient. Political freedom and economic independence went hand-in-hand.

The twentieth century was characterized by significant social, economic, and political change, especially in the wake of the Great Depression and World War II. However, even prior to these events, things were shifting. Industrial scale was increasing, people were moving into cities, and they were increasingly working for wages rather than farming for subsistence. Just a year before the Stock Market Crash of 1929, the Republican Party adopted a campaign slogan that encapsulated the emerging ideal: "a chicken in every pot and a car in every garage." Property was coming to be seen in terms of exchange and use rather than production. A person should be able to find work, and that work should pay a wage that would provide for a family's needs: chicken, a car, a garage, and so on. Rather than an emphasis on the ownership of capital that would make production possible, we see a shift toward wealth in the form of wages that would facilitate exchange. This signals a shift from the era of the free man, characterized by the ideal of productive property, to the era of exchange, characterized by the ideal of income for purchasing power. This shift brought with it a significant change—a constriction—in the idea of

18. Henry Louis Gates, Jr., "The Truth Behind '40 Acres and a Mule," *PBS* online.

freedom. Independence as an ideal—made possible by the ownership of productive property—was slowly eroded. The New Deal, for instance, sought to alleviate the suffering of the Great Depression by creating jobs. In the process Americans were aided in the short term, but it become much easier in the aftermath to imagine that the federal government, with its seemingly endless resources, would provide the ultimate security in a world that had become frightfully insecure and unpredictable. With FDR's Four Freedoms echoing in their ears, it became more natural to imagine that the government could, in fact, provide not only freedom of speech and worship but the hitherto unimagined freedoms from want and fear. The federal government came to be seen as the guarantor of economic security, and thus freedom moved from the independence facilitated by the ownership of capital to a good granted by the state.

Today this trajectory has led to the reinvigoration of socialism, which is a remarkable transformation wrought in less than two centuries. Where Tocqueville could remark in 1835 that in America "there are no proletarians," today the proletarian class constitutes a significant portion of the American populace. The citizen's relationship to property has continued to be transformed, and with it the concept of freedom has continued to shift. Where with the New Deal the federal government provided work so that Americans could earn an income and thereby purchase the goods they required, today the emphasis is not on state-provided employment but rather on state-provided services and a guaranteed income. The marriage of work and property—once exemplified by the ownership of productive property and then continued with wage labor—is being severed. What our modern socialists demand is a seemingly endless array of services: free health care, tuition-free college, and even "economic security for all who are unable or unwilling to work" as an FAQ sheet touting the Green New Deal put it before being hastily removed.[19] If you are "unwilling to work" you will continue to enjoy, not an income, not property, but "economic security."

Thus, we witness a steady decline: from productive property to income for the sake of purchasing consumables to, finally, the elimination of the necessity of work and the replacement of any notion of property ownership with the re-allocation of publicly funded and publicly administered services. Property, as an ideal that could inspire generations to strive toward securing it, has been replaced by state-provided services.

19. Ocasio-Cortez, *The Heartland Institute*, Feb. 8, 2019.

Unlimited government, run by "benevolent" plutocrats ostensibly working to provide all of the services citizens could desire, is replacing a government whose expansion was kept at bay by propertied citizens who
could provide for themselves and come to the aid of their neighbors.
Private property fosters the notion of limits, but as the aspirational language of both FDR's Four Freedoms and the Green New Deal indicate,
government services are open-ended and require the seemingly infinite
expansion of the state.

Chapter Seven

Virtue and Citizenship

How Property Makes Citizenship Possible

In the measure in which the number of independent people
shrinks and in which the large concern and mass organization
become typical of our times, in that same measure the market
economy loses some of it advantages over the collectivist
economy.

—WILHELM RÖPKE

IN A 1930 ESSAY titled "Economic Possibilities for our Grandchildren,"
John Maynard Keynes imagined a future when the economic problem
of scarcity would be solved by technology and compound interest, and
humans could then pursue more important things. But such a glorious
future would require economic growth, and in order to achieve that, we
must continue, for a time, to set virtue aside. "For at least another hundred years we must pretend to ourselves and to every one that fair is foul
and foul is fair; for foul is useful and fair is not. Avarice and usury and
precaution must be our gods for a little longer still. For only they can lead
us out of the tunnel of economic necessity into daylight." One day soon,
though, the "economic problem" will be overcome. We will, it would
seem, overcome the curse of the Fall, and work will be optional. Without
the need to live by the sweat of our brows, we will be free to pursue the

truly human things. At this point, Keynes grows rhapsodic: "I see us free, therefore, to return to some of the most sure and certain principles of religion and traditional virtue.... We shall honour those who can teach us how to pluck the hour and the day virtuously and well, the delightful people who are capable of taking direct enjoyment in things, the lilies of the field who toil not, neither do they spin."[1]

We hear in these words something of a precursor to the criticisms laid at the feet of modern capitalism by the Woke Socialists. Capitalism, they argue, is based in greed and aggressively corrodes virtue in individuals and in the society that embraces it. Capitalism fosters inequalities both economic and political. Capitalism is incompatible with a just society and must be replaced by an economic and social order that cultivates equality and justice.

Keynes was convinced that in order to sustain economic growth we must, for a time, embrace vice and deny virtue. We must set aside worship of God and continue to bow to the god of avarice. We must, in short, take up idols if our economy, as currently structured, is to remain healthy. But once we cross the threshold of plenty, we can make the switch to virtue. We can build a new world that truly reveals the possibilities in human nature that have hitherto been held at bay by economic demands.

Keynes wrote this in 1930. He anticipated that by 2030 the world would be fundamentally different. (2030 is also, incidentally, only a year prior to the end of the world if we take AOC's doomsday clock seriously.) In some striking ways the Woke Socialists believe that 2030 is now. They tell us that work is, or should be, optional. Virtue is possible, nay, almost guaranteed once we rid the world of competition, inequality, and greedy corporations run by white men intent on making a profit. They imagine a new world without scarcity, where medical costs and college tuition are paid for by someone else and where clean energy is in infinite supply. This vision of plenty is combined with a social agenda that would, no doubt, have shocked Keynes, who died before the sexual revolution of the 1960s.

Virtue has always been understood as, at minimum, the exercise of self-control, a willingness to defer physical pleasure rooted in appetitive desire for the sake of something higher, more noble, and more truly human. An obvious question: what if we are at a point where we can work less (and even imagine that work is unnecessary), but—contra Keynes—we don't take that opportunity to cultivate virtue? What if our newfound

---

1. Keynes, "Economic Possibilities for our Grandchildren."

freedom is used as a license rather than as an opportunity? What if we have forgotten that, at least initially, virtue is difficult and vice is easy? What if we come to speak only of our rights and not of our duties? We can ask similar questions in terms property: What sort of virtues are called forth by the ownership of real property? What sort of virtues are called forth by, say, the New Deal work programs? What sort of virtues are called forth by Woke Socialism? What if we come to demand services and freedom but fail to be shaped by the ownership of private property? What sort of citizens will we be? What sort of nation will we have? It is to the question of citizenship that I now turn.

Citizenship and Property

Today in America the question of citizenship is problematic. The discussion takes a variety of forms, and the intensity varies, but most Americans recognize at some level that things are amiss. Of course, the question of immigration brings out some of the themes and plenty of the hostility. Who should be allowed to come to America? Is illegal immigration a problem? Perhaps any border restrictions on immigrants are merely the imposition of rich white people afraid of losing their places of privilege and power. In 2019 the question of whether the U.S. Census should or could include a question about citizenship went all the way to the Supreme Court.[2]

But the problem of citizenship is not simply another way of framing a discussion about immigration. Set the immigration question aside, and citizenship remains an important issue, for the idea of citizenship turns on the assumption that something unifies us as a people. As we become increasingly polarized as a nation, it becomes increasingly difficult to identify precisely what it is that makes us *E pluribus unum*.

Citizenship implies some degree of commonality, something shared by all who claim the title "citizen." In most cases this includes sharing the same territory. Citizens live in the same place. They inhabit a common land, and that implies a state with borders, which may be relatively open or relatively restrictive. Citizenship has often been associated with a shared way of life that includes common ethnicity, language, and religion. In a pluralistic country, those binding agents are less powerful. In the United States the shared colonial experience—including the eventual

2. U.S. Supreme Court. Department of Commerce v. New York.

resistance against Great Britain—helped to unify the colonists. Unlike today, most Americans at the time of the American Founding were Protestant Christians, western Europeans, and small property holders.

Some have argued that America is a "creedal nation," or, as Lincoln put it, a nation "dedicated to a proposition." America, so goes the argument, is a unique experiment in which citizens are bound, not by ethnicity, religion, or culture but by a national creed embodied in The Declaration of Independence. We as Americans hold certain truths to be "self-evident," and these truths include a commitment to equality and the fact that all humans possess certain rights. We hold that government is a creation of the people, that it exists to protect the rights of all, and that its legitimacy is rooted in the consent of the governed. Americans, so it is argued, are unified in their affirmation of these basic principles. Citizenship, at its core, turns on a common national (not religious) creed or set of propositions. Anyone can become an American if only he affirms the truths articulated in the creed.

There are serious problems with this account of America and American citizenship. First, a simple national creed is inadequate. Those who argue that America is a creedal or propositional nation ignore an important fact. America was founded by people deeply formed by the Christian narrative who believed in a moral order that was both intelligible and obligatory. Jefferson's grand phrases about the "self-evident" truth that "all men are created equal, that they are endowed by their Creator with certain unalienable Rights, that among these are Life, Liberty, and the pursuit of Happiness," were written amid a cultural consensus that simply does not exist today. The propositions expressed in the Declaration of Independence provide an adequate framework of self-understanding only if they are superimposed upon a background of a shared cultural vision. Abstract propositions about the human condition are not adequate to bind a people to each other or to a common good. The idea of a propositional nation worked only when the propositions were not doing the heavy lifting required to form a people into citizens. The propositional nation was a shorthand—or, perhaps better, a sleight-of-hand—that exchanged the thick cultural consensus necessary to bind a people for glowing abstractions that have proven inadequate once the underlying consensus collapsed.

Even if we assume that American citizens were once bound by a common commitment to a common creed, that shared consensus has broken down. The common truths are no longer affirmed as common truths. Tocqueville argued that laws are an important part of what gives America its identity, but more fundamental than laws are the mores that give shape to the moral world. Tocqueville defines mores as "the whole moral and intellectual state of a people."[3] If the mores of a people change, or, perhaps more to the point, if the mores fragment so that groups holding competing sets of mores occupy the same territory and subsist under the same Constitution and the same founding propositions, we should expect political chaos. The rights to life, liberty, and the pursuit of happiness, once seen as gifts endowed to humans by their creator, have become problematic. Jefferson's concepts required a background consensus about the moral shape of the universe that ultimately includes a God by whom people are endowed with rights. Jefferson's language is also beholden to a Lockean conception of the person as an autonomous individual possessing natural rights in a state of nature prior to the formation of a civil society, which emerges through the consent of individuals for the sake of preserving their natural and God-given rights.

Today the underlying cultural, philosophical, and even theological consensus is gone. At the time of the Founding pluralism extended across a range of Protestant denominations along with a smattering of Catholics and Jews. The English language and English laws characterized the national culture (and most local cultures). Today the pluralism is much broader. Many Americans claim no religious affiliation, and those who are religiously committed are not limited to various Christian denominations. Instead, Muslims, Jews, Buddhists, Hindus, and many others call America home. And while English is still the majority language, there are many who do not speak English, and many state and local governments accommodate various language-speakers in the services they offer. The inadequacy of a common creed or commitment to a common set of propositions becomes increasingly obvious as American society becomes increasingly pluralistic. The binding agents are being lost, and when that happens the creedal language loses any effectiveness it once had. It goes without saying that the hackneyed claim that "our diversity is our strength" is patently false apart from a consensus that lies deeper than the diversity.

In the absence of a common religion, ethnicity, or even a common language, a strong sense of citizenship that creates the sense of a common enterprise or a common mission is difficult to achieve. Of course,

---

3. Tocqueville, *Democracy in America*, 275.

a common enemy might do the trick, but this means that the problem is merely suppressed until the enemy is defeated. Once that happens (as with the collapse of the USSR) the problem of pluralism emerges again.

Woke Socialism, for its part, seems to cultivate a sort of anti-citizenry. Authentic citizenship, at its core, must give birth to a sense of duty and a willingness to sacrifice for the common good. A citizen is one who loves his place and is even willing to suffer so that present and future citizens might enjoy the benefits of citizenship. This is only achievable if the vast majority of individuals see themselves as participating in a common endeavor and cherish the fact that they belong to a community of fellow citizens. Woke Socialism calls for nothing in the way of sacrifice. It promises radical social transformation paid for by "the rich" who are both an abstract presence and a concrete enemy. In so doing, a common citizenship is replaced by conflict that pits the poor and minorities (along with their political advocates) against the rapacious, greedy rich and their multi-national corporate enterprises. Citizenship is reduced to class warfare. One nation under God is transformed into the rich vs. the poor, or the woke vs. the unwoke, or the down-trodden and under-privileged vs. the well-off and privileged, or, as the Green New Deal puts it, "indigenous peoples, communities of color, migrant communities, deindustrialized communities, depopulated rural communities, the poor, low-income workers, women, the elderly, the unhoused, people with disabilities, and youth" vs. whoever is left, which, if we take this lineup literally, means: white men with jobs.

It might be that private property can help provide a common ground for citizenship in a pluralistic society. However, such a solution has no chance of working in the context of a plutocracy. At its root, democratic citizens must believe they are all playing the same game. They must believe that there is a common set of rules that apply to all. A plutocracy destroys that perception because it undermines the reality of commonality. It actively works to create advantages for some at the expense of all the rest. In short, plutocracy erodes the conditions necessary for healthy democratic citizenship.

A rigged system (recall that's how Bernie Sanders, Elizabeth Warren, and Charles Koch describe our current system) is inherently unjust. It is one where the notions of duty and responsibility are replaced by attempts to game the system by seeking to harness the state to create market advantages. And it here becomes obvious why a plutocracy naturally degenerates into a kleptocracy—rule by thieves. The response of those who do not have capital or access to power is to appeal directly to the state for free goods and services. Thus, plutocracy invariably creates clients of state power. Various groups seek to benefit themselves at the expense of fellow-citizens who have been reduced to adversaries in a competition for state resources and power.

Plutocracy superimposed on a democracy creates resentments that are legitimate and inequalities that are not. This is not to say that all inequalities are unjust. As I have noted, a free society will always include inequalities. Even if everyone began with equal holdings, inequalities would soon emerge if individuals are free to buy and sell their property. Some are more talented, more ambitious, more industrious, or luckier than others. However, inequalities that result from the free exchange of goods in a system that is not "rigged" to the advantage of some are far easier to tolerate than inequalities produced by a system rigged to favor some and disadvantage others.

Thus, inequalities are not always morally neutral and socially harmless. Again, citizens must have confidence that everyone is playing the same game. Everyone must acknowledge that there are duties and responsibilities that come with citizenship. This is true even in an aristocratic society where social inequalities are built into the system and are determined by birth. *Noblesse oblige*, the obligation of nobility, indicates that with the privileges of nobility comes the responsibility to care for those who are less advantaged. Inequalities are tolerable when the duties associated with aristocracy are observed. A decadent aristocracy is one in which men claim the privileges of status but ignore its responsibilities. Such a society is ripe for revolution.

In a democratic society the extreme inequalities natural to an aristocracy are less likely to be tolerated. However, since freedom naturally results in inequalities, it is helpful to ask: how much inequality is possible in a democratic society? Recall that Montesquieu argued that in a republic "extreme equality" was not possible nor is it a healthy goal. But neither is extreme inequality. In a "commercial republic" a significant amount of inequality can be tolerated because commerce helps citizens cultivate the virtues of restraint: self-control and frugality. But even then excessive inequality will eventually cause citizens to lose sight of each other. They will no longer rub shoulders and interact on a daily basis as equal citizens, for even if *economic* inequalities exist, citizens must still see themselves as *political* equals. A healthy democracy requires a commonality of the citizenry where each possesses the same formal access to power and each is confident that the rules apply equally to all. No one is so wealthy that his money can protect him from the law, and no one is so poor that he cannot access the machinery of justice. Again, plutocracy destroys this commonality, undermines trust in the system, and, by concentrating property, undermines a vital opportunity for the cultivation of virtue.

The American founders believed that a virtuous citizenry was a necessary condition for a healthy democracy (they called it a republic). Many, as we have seen, suggested that citizenship and property were tightly conjoined. Might it be that, in the absence of a common religion or ethnicity, a common commitment to the ownership of property could help foster the virtues necessary for healthy citizens?

Virtue and Property

The term "virtue" refers to one's character. A person of virtue is one who possesses the excellences of character that are proper to human beings. Obviously, this conception of virtue implies that there exists a common human nature that allows us to identify certain characteristics that an excellent person possesses. Prior to the nineteenth century this kind of claim was relatively uncontroversial. At the time of the American founding the language of virtue was widely employed, and though writers meant a variety of things by the term, nearly all affirmed the existence of a moral order created by God and to which humans were obligated. Even today, where metaphysical claims about human nature or moral reality are less widely affirmed, most of us recognize at some level the goodness of courage, self-control, wisdom, generosity, and so on. We praise people with such characteristics and we criticize those who are cowardly, feckless, foolish, and stingy.

The ownership of property is one means by which certain virtues necessary for a healthy and free society can be cultivated. Conversely, policies that undermine the institution of private property destroy an important venue in which the virtues are formed. How does private property aid in the formation of virtue? To answer this question, it is necessary to consider, briefly, how character is formed. Aristotle, that sensible Greek, taught that virtues are acquired through habit. Habits are formed through repetition until an action becomes "second-nature." When a person performs an action simply because "that's the way I do things," he has acquired a habit. The formation of habits often requires pain or discomfort. We (or our parents or some other authority figure) set up conditions to incentivize a particular behavior. At first we are uncomfortable, even miserable. But eventually we come to take pleasure in this new way of being and acting. When we come to find pleasure in the act (or when we find that not performing a particular act is unpleasant), we have formed a habit. Exercise is a good example. When we begin to exercise, it hurts. Everything in us screams to quit. To stay in bed. To continue on the path of least resistance, which means the couch with the Doritos. However, once we begin to experience the benefits of exercise, once our bodies (and minds) become accustomed to the new regimen, we feel bad when we *don't* exercise. Something has changed. A habit has been formed. Our character has taken on a particular shape.

The ownership of property can help shape virtues conducive to self-government, for when we exercise dominion over a piece of productive property, we are compelled to submit to limits imposed by the reality of the property. We are drawn into a context where our creativity is required, but we must also recognize that our creative efforts must conform to the contours of the particular property over which we have control. In simple terms, one cannot, through an act of creative will, make a hammer be a saw or turn a horse into a fish or compel a piece of land in Montana to grow banana trees. We must seek to understand the nature of the property we possess and work within the parameters of that nature if we are to be successful. In other words, we must learn the wisdom of limits. We must learn to see the world not simply as raw material upon which we can impose our infinitely creative wills but rather as consisting of particular things and places with particular potentialities and limits. In learning the wisdom of limits, we simultaneously learn to see opportunities latent in the world around us and more specifically in the property that we own.

The wisdom of limits is, in a way, a combination of two classical virtues: wisdom and self-control. We attain wisdom when we come to see the world more accurately. It is foolishness to seek to impose a false structure upon the world. It is lunacy to demand that the basic structure of the world be other than it is. Wisdom is accurately seeing and acting in accordance with reality. It is a kind of submission to the order of reality. Self-control is the ability to govern ourselves. Self-government is not, in its most basic form, a theory of politics or social power. Self-government in the political sense requires self-government in a more personal sense. Each of us must learn to govern our impulses, appetites, and desires. If we are habituated into incessantly demanding that our desires be satisfied by the state—in other words, if we behave like spoiled children—we are fundamentally ill-equipped for political self-government, for we have shown ourselves ill-equipped for personal self-government.

When a person owns productive property—that is to say, capital—there exists the opportunity to practice the art of self-sufficiency and with it the virtue of neighborliness. Productive property calls forth a variety of skills that are necessary for the maintenance and improvement of that property. Productive property requires work, intelligence, and the development of skills that can be put to use in a variety of contexts. When a person has the skills necessary to provide for himself, he is less inclined to look to the state for assistance. He may even develop a sort of fierce pride in his independence and steadfastly refuse to be seduced by the siren's song of goods and services from the omni-benevolent hand of the state. This self-sufficiency creates the ability to help one's neighbors. A community of interdependent neighbors, all equipped with various skills, tools, and capital, is far less likely to need state assistance than a "community" of individuals who lack the skills, resources, or the inclination to help their neighbors in need.

Jesus once remarked that "the poor will always be among you."[4] This means there will always be opportunities to help the less fortunate. This also implies the responsibility to do so. Those with property and skills, along with a character ordered by the virtue of generosity, are the ones best suited to help the poor.

When a person owns property that will either improve with care or diminish with neglect, the need to provide for oneself and one's family—or the desire to succeed more generally—will summon the virtue of responsibility. When property may be improved over time, one must attend to the painstaking work of planning for the future. With that, one must be willing to sacrifice pleasure, benefits, or leisure in the present for the sake of greater pleasure, benefits, or leisure in the future. The ability to defer gratification is, as any parent knows, a mark of maturity. It is not something that comes naturally to children, who generally need to be compelled or convinced to put off immediate gratification for a better future. Deferred gratification may be natural in ants and bees, but it comes much harder for most humans. The ownership of property can aid in this process.

4. Matthew 26:11.

Closely related to planning for the future is the virtue of thrift, an ideal that many Americans are forgetting as the Depression Generation passes off the scene. Some of us can recall parents or grandparents who obsessively saved every shred of paper and every scrap of food. They did this because they could remember years of scarcity. They knew first-hand what it was like to have less than enough, and those experiences shaped them profoundly. They knew how to make do, fix things, and do without. Montesquieu insisted that the virtue of frugality was vital for a healthy republic. A frugal person is one who cares well for his wealth and possessions. He is a good steward of his property. He is well-aware that circumstances are fragile and that a wise person will avoid lavish spending and care for his property to provide a buffer against hard times. Montesquieu believed frugality in citizens is an indicator of self-control and a pre-condition of self-government. A frugal person is one whose tastes run toward the simple rather than the lavish, who doesn't shy away from hard work, who is quite willing to sacrifice material comfort for the good of the community, and who expects the same of his fellow citizens.

All these might be called "middle-class virtues." As the young people today might put it, these are the "adulting" virtues: a bit boring, perhaps, but vital for successfully transitioning into the world of responsible adult-hood. These are not the heroic virtues. Instead, they are the day-to-day virtues necessary for a good, stable, and free society.

It is not hard to imagine a society consisting of citizens who do not possess some or most of these middle-class virtues. If citizens lack any notion of proper limits, of self-control, personal responsibility, or the ability or inclination to defer gratification for the sake of a better future, such a society would be gravely ill. In fact, such a society would seem to resemble nothing so much as a society of petulant children. As we have seen, a spoiled child needs, above all else, the firm hand of an adult. But in a society of spoiled children, who plays the adult? Obviously, the state most readily comes to serve that function, and the relationship is both mutually beneficial, mutually re-enforcing, and perverse, for unlike good parents who encourage their children to grow up, the state encourages perpetual childhood. The state wants, perhaps more than anything else, to expand its power and prerogative. This is a fundamental tendency of all political power. The state wants to expand, and a society of spoiled children demands to be cared for. But the state is never satisfied with its power, and spoiled children are never satisfied with the concessions and gifts of their enablers. Both want more, and they will get it, for both desire what the other can provide: the state wants power, and immature citizens want goods and services. It would seem to be a win-win situation with one small cost: freedom. And even this is cloaked behind an alluring mirage. A life without responsibility or a life without care for the future would seem to be a life of the most perfect freedom if, that is, perpetual childhood is the goal. However, freedom suited to a society of self-governing citizens requires more than a demand for an endless stream of publicly funded goods and services complemented by an endless stream of technological diversions. True freedom requires both the opportunity and inclination to think and live responsibly, to willingly sacrifice one's self for others, to plan for the future, to live within one's means, to fix and repair that which is broken, to celebrate the good gifts of hard work and commensurate reward in the company of friends and family to whom we are committed and who are committed to us. True freedom is not the absence of obligation or responsibility. It is not a life of endless pleasure and the avoidance of hard work. Freedom worthy of a society of self-governing men and women includes both sacrifice and service, without which freedom descends into the vortex of childish demands and the inevitable frustrations that ensue when those demands are not met.

The ownership of private property doesn't guarantee virtue nor does it guarantee freedom. It may be that other conditions are necessary for the benefits of property ownership to be fully realized. However, a society consisting of propertied citizens is more likely to foster the conditions for adulthood than any other. Thus, it would seem that when citizens no longer own property, they will very likely lose the opportunity to own property, and eventually they will lose the inclination to own it. They will, however, seek to alleviate their persistent sense of economic insecurity by looking to the only entity that seems powerful enough to help, namely, the state. And because property and power go hand-in-hand, concentrations of property lead inevitably to plutocracy. Thus, the decline of property ownership sets the stage for the dramatic expansion of personal vice and state power—a fundamentally unstable combination. It establishes the conditions that lead citizens to demand from the state what they once demanded from themselves. In the context of contemporary America, the decline of property ownership set the stage for Plutocratic Socialism, and the rise of the social justice movement gave this new iteration of socialism its distinctive "woke" flavor characterized by the revolutionary rhetoric, radicalism, and violence we are currently witnessing.

Chapter Eight

Privacy and Stewardship
Restoring Lost Ideals

And the LORD God took the man, and put him into the
garden of Eden to dress it and to keep it.

—GENESIS 2:15

The Diminishment of Privacy

WHEN WE THINK ABOUT private property, the emphasis is generally
on the "property" and we easily overlook the modifier "private." We do
well, however, to consider more closely the meaning of privacy and how
this has changed as our society has come to revolve increasingly around
services rather than property. When the "mineness" that characterizes
private property is replaced by the demand that my needs be sated by the
state, and when our attentions are diverted by the endless charms of our
electronic devices, we have entered into a new civilizational moment, a
moment that is no longer oriented to freedom or personal responsibility
but rather toward incessant demands couched in the language of rights.

Consider, in broad terms, how privacy has shifted. Americans increasingly live their lives "on-line." We seem increasingly willing and even
eager to display ourselves in ways that would make earlier generations
puzzled if not outright scandalized. Facebook seems to call forth a willingness in millions to share their lives with an array of "friends" who may

or may not resemble friends in any recognizable way. Through Facebook, Instagram, and other social media platforms we come to think of our "image" on-line as something that needs constant attention, a "personal brand" that we carefully curate so that those who encounter "us" (or the image of us) will be duly impressed with what they see. In the process the "self" comes to be less oriented to the private and more associated with the public, the disclosed, and the published. We seek to validate our experiences and thus validate our lives by capturing images and presenting them to the world via social media. If an experience is not presented on-line, did it really happen? Do such non-events really count in my attempt to cultivate an image that might make me an Influencer—that is, a person whose life and experiences are so interesting and well-presented that they influence the market decisions of others and can therefore be monetized?

With the rise of social media the realm of the private has dramatically diminished. When a mobile phone ad can intone that "I want to upload all of me," it is clear that we have entered into a new world where the private and the public are increasingly blurred and where the desire for the private has been replaced by the desire to exhibit ourselves as broadly and thoroughly as possible.[1] This urge reaches its apex (or perhaps its nadir) with internet pornography.

For generations sex was considered private. It occurred behind closed doors or in the dark. People generally understood sex to be deeply private, something the very nature of which would be altered if it were publicly displayed. This is not to say that sexual expressions or images were never presented in public. However, such expressions were generally shrouded in allusion or, if explicit, they were considered unseemly, crass, vulgar, and even barbaric. Today with the ubiquitous presence of internet pornography, the private has been made public, and with that shift porn has become increasingly mainstream, so that anyone who objects to the pornification of our cultural spaces (not to mention our little girls) is considered a prude who is "hung up" on Puritanical conceptions of sex that inhibit the free expression of sexual desire. As porn has insinuated itself into every aspect of our lives, the distinction between the public and private has become increasingly blurred. Social media and porn have similar effects on our understanding of privacy.

The technological attack on the private realm is also advancing in the name of security. New technologies are invariably presented as a

1. Sprint. "I am Unlimited," Jan. 31, 2013.

boon to consumers. The much-touted iPhone X offered consumers the benefits of facial recognition technology, making it impossible (or at least more difficult) for hackers to access their phones. Security cameras are increasingly common presences, recording activity on public streets to aid law enforcement in identifying criminals.

As we all know, helpful technologies can be misused, and it is just a matter of time before they are. However, once we become accustomed to enjoying the benefits of any technology, it becomes far more difficult to rein in the inevitable abuses. The number of security cameras that today are readily accepted in the name of security would have made a previous generation balk.[2] In Idaho, what is by some counts the most conservative state in the nation, facial recognition cameras have been installed in the Boise city hall. These cameras will be programed to identify individuals who are not permitted to enter the building.[3] Clearly this provides enhanced security measures and makes law enforcement easier. However, it is easy to imagine how such devices could be used to exclude political enemies or persons who hold views not approved by whoever programs the devices.

The coronavirus pandemic provided another avenue for the encroachment of surveillance technology. When worry about public health is elevated, a technological society will readily look for technological solutions. It is not hard to imagine a situation in which travel is limited to those who can provide proof of non-infection or admission to public spaces requires proof of vaccination. At the time of this writing, such measures are being contemplated widely and implemented in certain places. In the name of security, the freedom of citizens is made contingent on submitting to health checks and procedures. As with surveillance measures, the justification often seems reasonable and benign. However, in both instances, the possibility of abuse is immense, and the likelihood of eventual abuse is virtually certain.

These concerns are all the more justifiable when we consider that the direction of security-enhancing technologies is almost always one way. Rarely are they dialed back. They advance so steadily because we desire security. We desire security because we feel insecure. We feel insecure because we are constantly told that we are insecure (and sometimes that's true). Obviously, it is in the best interests of technology companies

2. Pasley, *Business Insider*, Dec. 6, 2019.
3. Carmel, *Idaho Press*, July 6, 2019.

to increase our sense of insecurity, for then we will be much more willing to accept violations of our privacy in the name of greater security. The market potential is immense. Of course, it may be that we really *are* less secure, but this is not easy to establish. Compared to most of the world and most of human history, we live incredibly secure lives. Most of us can go about our daily affairs with little regard for security. Why, then, the persistent sense of insecurity? Could it be that the ownership of private property and the independence that such ownership provides makes security less of a concern than freedom? Is a society shaped by private property less susceptible to the invasion of the private than a society where property and privacy have been replaced by services and security? I think the answer is obvious.

My claim that the realm of privacy has been seriously compromised must be qualified, for although we seem to be increasingly willing to forgo privacy for the sake of our social media profile, sexual titillation, and enhanced security, our society has constructed an edifice of claims centering on, ironically, privacy. The Supreme Court discovered a hitherto unnoticed "right to privacy" in justifying abortion in the *Roe v. Wade* decision (1973). Here privacy is rooted in the body and leads to assertions such as "It's my body, and I can do whatever I want with it." With this we witness a curious reversal of the argumentative trajectory that we saw with Locke. Locke, of course, justifies the acquisition and ownership of property on the basis of self-ownership: I own myself. Thus, I own my labor. Thus, I own that with which I have mixed my labor. Self-ownership is leveraged to extend ownership beyond the self. Locke is interested in justifying land acquisition in order to establish the legitimacy of private property. But today the right to privacy (a version of Locke's self-ownership) is not primarily employed in the service of the acquisition of land or other capital. Instead it is employed to justify the expansion of individual desires.

When bodies are freely exhibited as items of consumption and pleasure, the only thing that remains private is the capacity to choose. Choice, then, becomes the new abode of the private. The desire for productive property has been dramatically eclipsed by the demand for the elimination of all impediments to individual choice. And choice, in this context, seems to center on issues of sexual behavior: my body is my own, and I can do with it what I please. Abortion on demand is one logical outcome of this line of thought (so long as we don't think about the person being aborted). But this is only the beginning. If my body is my absolute possession, and I can do with it anything I please as long as I don't harm anyone else (a curiously arbitrary proviso), then whatever desires I have are legitimate simply because they are *mine*. The "mineness" of private property is reduced to the "mineness" of private desire. When the logic of desire comes to full bloom, the choice of what I do with my body extends to identity itself: I can *do* and *be* anything I desire. The language of individual desires masquerading as rights completely overshadows the language of natural limits, responsibility, or restraint. Impediments on my desire (whether external or internal) are illegitimate constrictions on my freedom. *My* body, *my* property, *my* rights, *my* choice. The refrain is hard to distinguish from the plaintive wails of a spoiled child.

The body, then, becomes the last bastion of privacy, the last remnant of private property but stripped of any norms that would shape and direct the use of that privacy or that property. The body in this new age becomes merely another instrument to be used to gratify whatever appetite is most aggressive. In this movement from property to services we witness the infinite expansion of freedom to pursue whatever my appetites demand. However, we quickly forget—if we ever knew—the warning expressed by Plato long ago: we are free only when we rise above our appetites and are not ruled by them. A person ruled by appetite is nothing more than a beast.

When the taste for private property is replaced by a desiccated conception of privacy reduced merely to personal desire, the realm of morality is reduced to an incessant demand that choice be respected and that services be provided to support my desires. In the process, the connection between property and work is lost. With the loss of work as a necessary corollary to property comes the diminishment of personal responsibility. In place of work comes choice. In place of responsibility comes petulant demands. It's not difficult to image how citizenship changes with this changing notion of both property and privacy. The state emerges as the best equipped to deliver on the demands of citizens whose appetites drive their agendas. Citizenship characterized by virtue in pursuit of a common good is lost. In its place steps the state—aided by Big Tech—serving as both facilitator of ever-expanding desires and ultimately as umpire between competing desires.

In this age of Woke Socialism we are witnessing the rise a new kind of citizen: the liberated Gnostic nomad. He is liberated, for he insists that the only limits on free choice are those that he has explicitly chosen. He is Gnostic, for he sees the body as nothing more than an object, a means for the gratification of desire. He is a nomad, for he sees the entire world as the venue in which he can exercise this new and intoxicating freedom. He has little affection for the limits of particular places and little patience for the impositions of particular neighbors, fellow citizens, or even responsibility for the most helpless among us. The body has become merely an object of transitory consumption, and this orgy of desire is wrapped up in the psychic noise of social justice and climate crisis, which energizes the expansion of the state that promises to meet all of our demands: economic equality, the eradication of racism, sexism, and patriarchy, and salvation from the coming climate apocalypse.

Stewardship or Ownership?

When privacy comes to be understood primarily in terms of private desires expressed in sexual terms, a couple of things become painfully obvious. First, the notion of privacy has constricted dramatically. A vision of flourishing, responsible, and self-controlled citizens is replaced by impatient individuals demanding the free expression of their every desire. Second, and implied in the first, the virtues called forth by the ownership of productive property—virtues proper to free citizens—tend to be replaced by vices better suited to children in need of a master.

There is an obvious solution: the restoration of the idea of private property that includes more than the body and its capricious appetites. We need to reinvigorate the notion that property is fundamentally tied to work, personal responsibility, and oriented toward the full flourishing of human beings. But perhaps at the same time it would be helpful to reconsider ownership. Perhaps there are some ways of conceiving of ownership that are healthier than others. What I'm getting at is this: the way we think about private property changes dramatically if we think in terms of stewardship rather than in terms of what we might call "absolute ownership." The basic contours of the latter are obvious. My claims are absolute. What I possess is mine without qualification. I can do with my property whatever I choose. The horizon of my concerns extends no further than the horizon of my own life or the duration of my desires. Property, then, is seen primarily as a means by which I am satisfied. My concern for it, therefore, is limited to the span of my life or the perceived range of my needs. In this sense, private property is reduced to disposable terms: I will use my property for my own pleasure and, ideally, my life and my property will be used up at the same time, for to be alive without property is undesirable, but to not use up my property in my own life is a waste of potential pleasure.

Many, however, have understood the ownership of private property in dramatically different terms. What if all that we possess is held in trust? What if we are better conceived as stewards rather than absolute owners? What if ownership, properly conceived, calls forth a sense of responsibility that extends beyond our own desires and even beyond our own lives? Conceiving property in terms of stewardship provides a remarkably rich alternative to the prevailing view of ownership.

This alternative view of ownership can even find justification in the work of Locke, who is often associated with a doctrine of absolute ownership. Locke argues against suicide because we are God's workmanship and therefore He owns us. To destroy ourselves would be to destroy property belonging to another.[4] Of course, as Locke continues to develop his account of property, the ownership of God grows much dimmer and the exclusive right to own and dispose of property becomes more firmly rooted in the individual. However, his initial impulse to ground the limits of ownership in a theological claim represents a residual idea from Christian history.

Thomas Aquinas, for his part, argues that God is the owner of all property, and humans enjoy ownership as a trust. We care for property that has been entrusted to us as a way of tending the Creation, which is a basic task to which all humans are called. Aquinas argued that things are better cared for when particular individuals are responsible for them.[5] The so-called tragedy of the commons is rooted in a profound insight into human nature: we care for things more attentively and effectively when we have exclusive right to them. *Private* property, in other words, helps to preserve property. When property is held "in common" the all-to-human tendency is to treat it with less care (someone else will do it) or to seek to extract wealth from it before someone else does (first come, first served). In both instances the long-term health of the property is jeopardized by short-term thinking. Exclusive right to a piece of property provides a more effective means to ensure that the long-term health of the property is preserved and even enhanced. When that is the case, property owners

4. Locke, *First Treatise*, §86; *Second Treatise*, §6.
5. Aquinas, *Summa Theologica*, II-II, Question 66, Art. 2.

are better equipped to help those in need, which according to Aquinas and the entire Christian tradition is an unavoidable moral duty.

It may seem odd, or even confused, that in a book championing private property I would advance a notion that seems to qualify ownership. It might even imply a deeply limited conception of ownership. If property is held in trust, the vital key at the center of this idea seems to be responsibility to God rather than the absolute freedom to do with the property whatever I desire. If property and freedom are intimately linked, this would suggest that freedom and responsibility are intimately linked as well. This represents, at the very least, a far more complex notion of freedom than one rooted only in private desire.

However, it may not be that understanding property ownership in terms of stewardship requires the theological justification that I have suggested. It may be possible to think of stewardship as a responsibility to future generations rather than a responsibility to God. If I conceive of my property as something I hold in trust for future generations, my decisions and actions must be characterized by a sober attention to the future rather than exclusive attention to my present enjoyment. When my temporal horizons are extended beyond my own life, when I come to assume responsibility for individuals not yet even born, I will come to think of my property as something for which I am obligated to care rather than something I am free to use up or destroy. When property is viewed in this light, we can see how what we called the middle-class virtues can be cultivated by shifting our temporal horizons. Responsibility, self-control, planning for the future, and thrift emerge as necessary qualities if we find ourselves attending to the needs of those future persons, most of whom we will never live to meet.

The trick, of course, is cultivating this way of thinking about the future. Conceiving of God as the proper owner of everything and humans as His stewards tasked with cultivating those things entrusted to us provides the moral framework for a doctrine of stewardship. A non-theological conception of responsibility can provide the same impetus, but generating a concern for the future beyond our own lives is more difficult, though perhaps not impossible. Plenty of non-religious people intuitively grasp the fact that they are stewards and seek to live their lives accordingly. Obviously, the justification for care must be reconsidered apart from theological commitments, for the language of stewardship seems to imply that one has been tasked with responsibilities by a superior. While God fills the role of superior and therefore anchors a coherent account of stewardship, a non-religious conception must find another justification. One could, for instance, personify nature as an authority or simply assume the structure of stewardship absent any lines of authority. However, when nature is tasked with serving the role of God, it is clear that we have not jettisoned a religious view but merely shifted the locus of authority. On the other hand, if we deny any authoritative structure to our conception of stewardship, we find ourselves assuming responsibility but doing so in a way that denies the internal logic of stewardship while attempting to maintain the positive outcomes. This, of course, is far better than denying any notion of stewardship. But while the practical consequences may exist without the theological foundation, it is not entirely clear that this is a long-term solution or merely a short-term fix that depends on a residual theological memory. Once the residue dissipates, one wonders if any strong view of stewardship is possible.

Thus, stewardship provides us with an approach to private property that avoids the extreme of absolute ownership (resulting in possessive individualism or careless consumption) on the one hand and communal ownership (resulting in the tragedy of the commons) on the other. Both extremes undermine the sense of responsibility that is so necessary for the long-term care of property.

Stewardship leads us to see the world as a gift to be cared for responsibly with an eye to the future. When we come to think of all that we possess as a gift, our view of the world is radically transformed, for all that we possess then calls forth a disposition of gratitude. The material things we are called to steward—even those things we earn by the sweat of our brows or the cleverness of our minds—take on a different appearance. We own material things so that we can provide for ourselves, our families, and our neighbors. We care for these material things knowing that we have been tasked with the responsibility of using them in a way that benefits others. Wanton disposability grates hard against this way of seeing material possessions. When we come to see our possessions as gifts held in trust, we are naturally oriented to think in terms of preservation of things that can be preserved and careful use of things that cannot. Responsibility, self-control, recognition of limits, and thrift come to characterize our approach to possessions.

This view of property will shape our thinking and acting in ways that extend beyond simple material possessions. In fact, the way we view the natural world, our cultural inheritance, and even our own bodies will be transformed when we come to see ourselves as stewards. This, in turn, will color the way we think about many of the major issues of our day.

The Natural World

We did not create the natural world, but we can care for it—and even improve it—or we can exploit it and reduce its beauty and health. The natural world is the source of food, water, and building materials as well as beauty and entertainment. It is not impervious to abuse. We can diminish the health and vitality of the natural world by reckless extraction of resources, careless use, and a willing disregard for the delicate balances that characterize good stewardship. If we ignore the limits inherent in the natural world, if we insist that it submit to our unlimited desires, we may for a time enjoy the benefits of that accelerated use, but in the end, the natural world will assert itself, and the debts incurred by our irresponsibility will come due. We, or our descendants, will pay for our hubris. Stewardship of the natural world means living responsibly within limits that wise people seek to understand but fools ignore or deny.

Climate change is, perhaps, the most intensely discussed issue today pertaining to the natural world. Yet rather than approaching the topic in terms of wise stewardship, the conversation oscillates between hysteria and denial. Both positions are unhelpful and offer little of substance. "Climate deniers" are reproached as willfully blind individuals who don't "believe" in the "settled science" that proves that the climate is changing. Such rhetoric traffics in inquisitional language and suggests that "deniers" are heretics that must be re-educated or purged. On the other hand, skeptics of climate change argue that "global warming" advocates are foisting a hoax upon the naïve by inciting a crisis to seize power. An ethic of stewardship would avoid either extreme and seek to ask and answer basic questions with an eye to responsible, long term action. Some basic questions: 1) Is the climate changing? Unless we assume that climate is perpetually static, it seems reasonable to assume that climates naturally change over time. 2) Are temperatures rising? It seems that most data—though not all—suggest that they are, although establishing a global average temperature is not simple nor without controversy. 3) Are rising temperatures caused by human activity? This is more difficult to assess, but rapid increases in average temperatures that correspond with the rise of industrialization suggests that humans have contributed, at least in part, to rising temperatures. 4) Are rising temperatures a bad thing? Of course, we hear of extreme weather, drought, fires, loss of coastal land, etc. caused by rising temperatures. We are constantly informed of the dangers of rising temperatures. It would be useful to at least consider if there are any benefits. For instance, can food be grown more efficiently in some places now that temperatures are higher? Asking the question will equip us to evaluate more adequately the net gains and net losses, both of which likely exist. 5) If we determine that increasing temperatures are caused by human activity, and if those changes result in a net loss, then we should seek ways to slow or reverse the trend if possible. This may require individuals to change some aspects of their lives. It might require that nations take on the task of facilitating some of those changes through incentives or even the coercion of law. But beware of self-righteous wielders of power who are eager to coerce others even as they exempt themselves. When that happens, one can rest assured that climate change rhetoric is a mask for a power grab. Of course, dramatically reducing or even eliminating carbon emissions would require revolutionary changes to our economy and infrastructure. The scope of the problem is massive. Ignoring or glossing over the scale, impact, and pain of the proposed solutions is both dishonest and ultimately ineffective. 6) The practical politics of reversing the upward trend of temperatures becomes especially complicated when we consider that without China and India committing to the enterprise, there are limits to what can, in fact, be done. Ultimately, a good steward will not be deterred by the complexity of the issues, but will, instead, work diligently to seek wise solutions in a way that exhibits neither hysteria nor carelessness.

With all that, the climate conversation should not blind us to the simple, practical ways we all can practice good stewardship of the natural world in our daily lives. The magnitude of some perceived problems can induce paralysis and even despair. Yet faithful stewardship must always be born out of hope, humility, and wisdom. Humility and wisdom must help us see that dependence upon centralized solutions may actually contribute to the problem of centralized power that is ubiquitous in our globalizing age. Good work characterized by loving attention to our particular places is the necessary first step to caring for the natural world as a whole. Ignoring our local places in the name of global abstractions is foolishness and will in the end leave us only with broken and ugly places.

Our Cultural Inheritance

When we understand ourselves as stewards, we will see ourselves as inheritors of cultural and political goods that must be cultivated if they are to survive. Civilization is not automatic. A free society is not natural. In fact, political freedom is a remarkable achievement. It requires generations of sacrifice, experimentation, discipline, and practice. In America we are inheritors of an English tradition in self-government that developed over centuries. The Magna Carta and the English Bill of Rights—not to mention the Bible—stand behind our own Declaration of Independence and Constitution. Our founding documents are unimaginable apart from the principles and practices articulated and fostered by what preceded them. Today when we enjoy the blessings of freedom, we are enjoying good things bought at a high price. We are enjoying benefits purchased by sacrifices willingly made by our forebears in the hopes that their offspring would be free. When we take those things for granted, when we act as if political freedom is a natural occurrence or simply a right that can be demanded, when we act as if living in a free society entails only benefits to be enjoyed and no responsibilities to be born, we are consuming finite cultural capital, and it is only a matter of time before our freedoms disappear. Stewardship of our cultural and political inheritance means living gratefully and responsibly in such a way that our institutions are strengthened and by inculcating in ourselves and our children the habits and practices necessary for sustaining and improving that which we have inherited. To ignore the need to care for our institutions and practices is to squander the very things that make a free society possible.

In light of the delicate nature of a free society, it becomes clear that each generation is responsible for educating its replacement. If we fail in this process of transmission, our freedoms will quickly dissipate. Thus, to be ignorant of our history and the principles and practices that constitute our way of life and our political order is to forfeit the very things that make us who we are. Moreover, the attempt to rewrite or destroy our history is, at heart, an act of radical ingratitude. This disposition characterizes the Woke Socialists, who are intent on teaching American school children that their country is unambiguously evil and that revolution is the only path to true justice.

The recent enthusiasm for education in the STEM fields is admirable and, in many ways, necessary; however, there is a significant difference between a person highly educated in mathematics, for instance, and a person who understands math in the larger context of the liberal arts. A liberal education, at its best, is an education in the art of being free. It is an education in the art of self-government. A properly conceived liberal education is one oriented toward asking fundamental questions about what it means to be human. It seeks to articulate the best sort of life and the best sort of society in light of unchanging facts of human nature. When a person pursues a STEM field education with a prior foundation in the liberal arts, she possesses the resources necessary to recognize the proper limits of science and its technological offspring. She becomes equipped to ask what "ought" to be done rather than simply becoming intoxicated with the possibilities of what "can" be done. In other words, a liberal education equips a person with a moral vocabulary and a moral framework that serve to direct and limit the power latent in our technological innovations. The Founders of America were liberally educated individuals who understood that government is not reducible to technique and that humans are not simply a bundle of desires. Instead, government is an art that requires practical wisdom born of experience and a deep understanding of human nature. Humans are complex creatures whose base desires need to be ordered by reason and whose habits should be derived from moral truths and religious commitments. An education that ignores these truths and commitments, or, what is worse, an education that denies that such things even exist, undermines the complex array of freedoms we have inherited.

This account of education has implications for the immigration debate that currently besets our national conversation. If a free society depends on a common foundation of ideas and practices that, at least in part, are inculcated through education, an immigration policy that ignores the necessity of educating immigrants is a policy that will undermine American freedom. Immigration without assimilation is a failure to recognize, at the level of policy, the need to steward responsibly that which we have inherited and to pass on those goods to current and future citizens. Immigration without assimilation is the same, in practical terms, as failing to educate the next generation in the ideas and practices that constitute who we are. It is suicide by neglect.

When we think in terms of stewardship it becomes painfully obvious that a policy of open borders (something being pushed by the Woke Socialists as well as some libertarians) represents a dereliction of the duty of citizenship. One aspect of stewardship is to love and care for one's country. This is central to the idea of patriotism. But love requires knowledge and time. Ultimately, if the survival of a nation requires the assimilation of immigrants into a particular cultural and political way of life, the removal of borders or unrestricted immigration will necessarily destroy a nation.

Bodies

Finally, the disposition of stewardship has implications for how we view our own bodies. If we are wise enough to admit that we are not self-created, then we must eventually come to recognize that we are born with debts we can never repay. Is my existence—my very being—something I possess as property or is it a gift to be faithfully stewarded? If my identity is simply my possession, then I can, ostensibly, alter my identity limited by nothing other than my desire. If my body is simply my possession, then I can use it as I use any other tool or implement. However, if my being is a gift, the duty to treat the gift responsibly becomes apparent. If my body is a gift, I am responsible to steward it well. Once again we are flirting with theological categories, for gift implies a giver, and while we can, perhaps, thank previous generations for the gift of a cultural inheritance, it is not as clear that the same requirement of gratitude extends to our bodies or our being more generally. Our existence is on one level due to certain biological facts and acts over which we had no say and which could seem to require little in the way of gratitude or responsibility. However, if we see our being as a gift from God, then we necessarily will come to see our bodies as part of this gift. Bodies must be respected because they have been given to us by God, and, presumably, He has built in certain limits and directions that are proper to His gift. Suicide is, from this perspective, a failure to treat the gift of life with the respect and gratitude it deserves. So, too, self-mutilation. Murder along with physical, sexual, and psychological abuse are likewise acts that deny the basic giftedness of being. Stewardship implies proper care of ourselves and of others, for, yes, we are our brother's keeper.

This approach to bodies and, by extension, to identity, has obvious implications for some of the most divisive social issues of our day. If identity is a gift, then the claim that gender is fluid and determined primarily by desire or personal preference is, simply put, a lie. If maleness and femaleness are gifts, then we are not simply free to attempt to alter the nature of the gift. Our identity is a gift to be stewarded, even if that task is difficult. If bodies are a gift, then they are to be treated with dignity and respect. If maleness and femaleness are gifts, then the differences between male and female should be appreciated and preserved. If this is true, then the fact that females can conceive and bear children should not, as is so often the case, be seen as a lamentable burden. Rather, fertility should be seen as a remarkable gift to be cherished and even celebrated. In this light, abortion is a denial of the goodness of the gift of femaleness—it is anti-woman. It is also a willing destruction of the being and body of another. It is an act of hostility where hospitality is called for. It is a denial of the gift of fertility and the gift of life granted to another. It is an abdication of the responsibility entailed in begetting another person.

The debates around sex, gender, and reproduction look dramatically different depending on how we view our bodies. If we view our bodies as absolute possessions with which we can do anything we desire, it would appear that any sexual expression is equally good (as long as it's consensual), sex changes are perfectly legitimate, and abortion on demand is simply a right. However, if we approach our bodies as gifts that must be stewarded with care and responsibility, we will likely come to very different conclusions.

Ultimately, the way we relate to the natural world changes when we approach environmental questions from the perspective of stewardship. Likewise, we will better care for our institutions and cultural inheritance when we see these through the lens of stewardship. So, too, our vision changes when we see the human body—and identity itself—as a good to be respected and gratefully cared for rather than simply another item to be used and consumed. Property ownership teaches us how to be good stewards. It is a practical school of stewardship whose lessons extend far beyond economics. Understanding our relationship to the world, to our culture, and to ourselves in terms of stewardship changes everything.

Chapter Nine

Conclusion

Renewing Property to Renew America

> If we are serious about reducing government and the burdens
> of government, then we need to do so by returning economic
> self-determination to the people.
>
> —WENDELL BERRY

A CENTURY BEFORE THE demise of the Roman Republic, two brothers held the position of tribune. During his years in military service, Tiberius Gracchus (died 133 B.C.) gained a reputation as an honest and coura-geous man. After serving abroad he returned to Rome to find that the lands of the poor were being summarily appropriated by the wealthy, thus leaving the masses bereft of property and increasingly dependent. To prevent the accumulation of land into a few hands, he proposed a law prohibiting anyone from owning more than five hundred jugera (about 311 acres). The wealthy attempted to ignore this law that directly limited their ability to concentrate property. Tiberius also promoted a series of policies to reduce poverty and dependence by encouraging ownership of land. He was accused of seeking undue power, provoked the ire of the wealthy, and was assassinated.

Gaius Gracchus (died 121 B.C.) soon came to power. He was broadly supported by the common people and generally opposed by the wealthy. Like his brother, he promoted agrarian land reforms. In an attempt to

130

solidify his power, he launched a series of spending initiatives geared toward appeasing the people and undermining the power of the Senate. He built roads, granted the franchise to all Italians, and subsidized the price of grain (sound familiar?). This worked for a time, but his opponents soon copied his methods, promising even more goods and services from the public treasury. Eventually, his support crumbled and he, like his brother, was assassinated.

The account of the Gracchus brothers is found in Plutarch's *Lives of the Noble Greeks and Romans,* which was widely read at the time of the American Founding.[1] As the founders contemplated forming a new nation, these and other stories from antiquity haunted their imaginations. In a remarkable way, the same dilemma faced by the Gracchi confronts us today. We can either attempt to revitalize private property by seeking to expand property ownership or, alternatively, we can attempt to employ the power and the resources of the state to appease the propertyless masses. Today a few leaders advocate—at least in their rhetoric— the first option. But most, including the Woke Socialists, seem deeply committed in practice to the second. It's sobering to note that both alternatives led, in the ancient world, to violence and bloodshed.

However, just because both Gracchi brothers met with a violent end does not mean that their agendas were equal. The American constitutional order depends on the existence of propertied citizens who are self-governing, who possess virtues like self-control, an ability to plan for the future, and who look to themselves, their neighbors, and God—not the state—for their daily bread. Today the Plutocrats are consolidating their power, and in response to perceived injustices rooted in inequality the Woke Socialists openly advocate a total transformation of the American landscape. In the name of social justice, they are advancing policies that, if successfully instituted, would further contribute to the infantilization of the American populace and the denigration of self-government. These revolutionaries don't naturally speak the language of property, independence, or duties. Instead, like the Jacobins of the French Revolution, they speak in terms of expanding government services, taxing the rich, radical equality, and the infinite expansion of individual rights with little attention to correlative duties.

1. See Nash, *Books and the Founding Fathers,* 12.

From Careful Owner to Caring State

In light of these concerns, we might be tempted to simply champion the restoration of productive property. But as we have seen, throughout most of human history the quintessential form of property has been land. To attempt to devise a political program around the idea that Americans should once again be land owners is clearly a non-starter. There is not enough land to accomplish this in any meaningful way. And furthermore, many Americans have no interest in owning land. If this is case, then a revitalization of property must, at the very least, include a reconceptualization of property that would include forms of productive property other than land.

However, we must acknowledge the difficulty of our current situation. Shifting conceptions of property have important, though perhaps not obvious, social effects. For instance, when property was conceived primarily as productive land, owners could improve their property over time and in the process increase the value of their property and improve their economic situations. Productive land (at least on a modest scale suited to the personal attention of the owner) provides a constant, tangible reminder of the connection between property, work, and independence. Political liberty is an embodied extension of the principles required to live and work on one's own land. Jefferson's dictum about the yeoman farmer, though lacking nuance, did point to an important truth. Property and freedom go together. Owning productive property tends to cultivate *careful owners* who jealously guard their property and jealously guard their liberty.

But as we have seen, property is no longer conceived primarily in terms of land. If we think of property today, we tend to think in terms of abstract wealth and consumer goods—cash, stocks, and 401ks on the one hand, and cars, boats, and shoes on the other. Our wealth makes it possible to purchase a variety of labor-saving devices and toys—items whose purpose is to make our lives easier or to entertain us. Rather than thinking of property as something that must be improved over time through persistent hard work, we tend to think of property as something that can be immediately enjoyed, and when it falls into disrepair or no longer serves its purpose, we discard it and purchase a replacement. This way of thinking is exacerbated by the planned obsolescence built into many of our most coveted technologies. Long-term stewardship of the latest iPhone makes little sense when it will be useless in only a few short years.

We cultivate the habit of using things up, disposing of them, and buying the latest shiny version. When we think of property primarily in terms of wealth and consumption, the careful owner readily becomes the *careless consumer* whose temporal horizons extend only as far as the immediate enjoyment provided by the toys we purchase (often on credit).

In this age of Plutocratic Socialism, we continue to move further away from the ideal of broadly owned productive property. This step is not surprising, for the state, at the behest of the people, seeks to alleviate the insecurities that a consumerist society tends to foster. In a propertied society, citizens are oriented toward independence and self-government, but a society of insecure consumers is going to demand security and services. The state emerges as the only entity capable of offering the array of services demanded by bored and insecure consumers. This dynamic is an ideal match. Citizens quickly become accustomed to looking to the state to satisfy their various needs and desires, which become increasingly difficult to distinguish. The state offers up the full weight of its resources to meet the ever-expanding demands of the citizens who will vote for the party and candidates that promise the most services. The state emerges as the generous provider. The careless consumer is perfectly complemented by the *caring state*. But the "care" has strings attached: services require obedience to rules and regulations. And what is perhaps even more insidious, a society oriented around the pursuit of apparently limitless state services will, perhaps invariably, become a society in which everything becomes politicized. When the state is summoned to meet our every need (and every desire), we come see all of life through the lens of political power. Property, responsibility, limits, restraint, and planning for the future are replaced by an incessant demand for services with little concern for financial limits, personal restraint, or any thought for the future.

We are in a precarious situation, and it is not at all clear that we will proceed in a way that is favorable to freedom. In so many ways, the momentum is moving in the wrong direction. Plutocratic Socialism is both helping to create the momentum and capitalizing on it. The major components of this shift are not difficult to discern. Too many Americans have lost the taste for real property and have come to desire consumer goods and government services instead. With that shift has come a decline in the social and psychological conditions necessary for a healthy conception of freedom. Today, many Americans are economically insecure. Events such as the 2008 economic collapse and the 2020 coronavirus lockdowns decimated savings, destroyed small businesses, and positioned the state to ride in as savior. Rather than alleviating the insecurity by seeking to acquire productive property, citizens have been habituated to look to the state for economic as well as political security. Independence as an ideal and aspiration is being replace by dependence as a fact. As a result, citizenship has come to be seen as primarily a means to access services rather than an opportunity to serve the common good. Insecure, proletarianized citizens are ripe for revolutionary movements that promise immediate gratification of desires at the expense of the wealthy who have, ostensibly, gamed the system. This is the persistent danger of a plutocratic system overlaid on a democratic society charac-terized by a commitment to equality. Plutocrats must forestall the revo-lution while paying lip service to equality and democracy and feigning support for populist movements and socialist policies.

Recall the strategy expressed by Marx: the first step in the revolution is for the proletariat class to "win the battle of democracy." The simple requirement for the success of this strategy is to ensure that a major-ity of citizens are insecure and propertyless. Once that occurs, insecure and propertyless citizens will quite reasonably vote for candidates and policies that promise the security and services for which they long. Plu-tocrats will champion socialist policies as a way to mollify the masses and thereby maintain their own power. The stark political divisions that now characterize our nation are, in large measure, a contest between 1) the Plutocrats who are seeking to hold and expand their power, 2) the Woke Socialists championing expansive government programs and ultimately a revolution that would fundamentally reconfigure the nation, and 3) those who still believe in the ideals that underlie the American constitutional order. But this is not simply a contest between three competing factions, for the first two are natural, though perhaps surprising, allies. The fact of plutocracy creates insecure and propertyless citizens, which provides the impetus for the rise of socialism. The socialists want a revolution, and the plutocrats want to stay in power. Because in a democratic age political legitimacy is inseparable from a commitment to equality, the plutocrats are compelled to feign support for the revolution while actively working to thwart its success by expanding services and thus encouraging depen-dency. Thus, in terms of rhetoric and superficial policy, the plutocrats and the socialists work for the same goal even though the plutocrats si-multaneously work to moderate the revolution. Of course, this strategy is risky, for it could simply energize the revolutionaries unless they can be diverted with bread and circuses and frightened into submission with the threat of global pandemics, social instability, and climate conflagrations.

If, as I have argued (and the Founders assumed), our constitutional republic was built for a population of "middling" property owners, the numbers are not encouraging. According to the Pew Research Center, "the hollowing of the American middle-class has proceeded steadily for more than four decades." In 1971, 61 percent of Americans were in the middle-class, which represents a clear majority. By 2015, 50 percent were middle-class, with growth occurring both at the upper and lower ends.[2] A growing under-class will exert increasing political pressure on their plutocratic masters as insecure citizens look to the state to provide what the economy has not. The plutocrats, looking for clients to help maintain them in their wealth, will make common cause with the insecure proletarian class. It's a match made in heaven (or somewhere else). The political power of the plutocratic class will be facilitated and energized by a continually growing class of insecure clients demanding security and services. A healthy, vibrant majority of middle class citizens is the only means by which this dynamic can be thwarted.

An Ethic of Stewardship

Productive property and the habits of mind fostered by that property are essential complements to a nation of free and responsible citizens. But if a nation of yeoman farmers is no longer possible, we must reconceive property and responsibility in a way that meets the needs of our current situation. How? We must revitalize the ideal of the *careful owner*, and this can only be done when we come to think of ourselves as stewards. When we do so, our temporal horizons are pushed beyond the narrow confines of our immediate desires or even our individual lives. We will come to see our property (and this can include productive property, a home, the natural world, our institutions, our bodies, and even consumer goods) as held in trust. We are responsible to care for our property in a way that will improve it for those who come after us, for unlike absolute owners, stewards must always be mindful of future citizens—many not yet born—who will one day assume stewardship of our property, institutions, and nation. The duty of stewardship calls forth virtues of personal responsibility, self-control, thrift, and concern for others. These are the

2. *Pew Research Center*, Dec. 9, 2015.

virtues that a nation of self-governing citizens must possess if freedom is to flourish.

When we come to understand ourselves as stewards, several things come to light. First, land as the quintessential form of productive property becomes less essential. Stewardship applies to a wide array of goods—anything durable enough to persist in time can either be stewarded well or poorly. This include various forms of private property, but it also includes cultural gifts such as stories, songs, and celebrations. It includes institutions and practices that have been developed over time and passed from one generation to the next. Second, an ethic of stewardship will tend to awaken the desire to own property. Stewards are caretakers. The natural condition of a caretaker is to possess something to care for. The desire to possess durable property is the natural corollary of individuals animated by an ethic of stewardship. Third, stewards understand themselves as owing multiple debts of gratitude to past generations and, simultaneously, recognize a duty to future generations to steward well the gifts they have received. A steward is constituted by a complex and ongoing pattern of gratitude and obligation. In this respect, a steward's life is framed primarily by a sense of duty rather than an incessant demand for an ever-expanding assortment of rights. Finally, because stewards understand themselves as part of an ongoing process of care and transmission, they will see themselves as participants in a sweeping story rather than merely as atomistic blips without meaningful connection to either the past or the future. An ethic of stewardship, in other words, provides an important source of meaning—of belonging—for those who embrace it.

Of course, property ownership *per se* does not necessarily demand an ethic of stewardship. Absolute ownership can induce an individual to think only in terms of extraction and desire. However, property ownership, when attended with a proper disposition, can call forth an ethic of stewardship. At the same time, an ethic of stewardship can cultivate a desire to acquire and care for private property. The two work in tandem: an ethic of stewardship induces a person to acquire and care for property, and the ownership of property helps to stimulate an ethic of stewardship.

Policy for Property

Thus, at the level of personal morality, the idea of stewardship is an indispensable ingredient for a sustainably free society. However, as the

advocates of socialism offer their seductive wares to an increasingly proletarianized populace, it is worth considering public policy measures that
could help reverse this course.

First, it is absolutely essential that all citizens play the same game.
When people as different as Elizabeth Warren, Bernie Sanders, and
Charles Koch agree that the game is rigged in favor of some and to the
detriment of others, we should take notice. Regulations and tax laws
must not provide special advantages to the plutocrats and their lackeys.
A rigged system destroys trust and encourages cynics and gamers. Such
a system becomes not a framework for justice but a means of gaining
personal advantages.

Second, policies must be ordered toward encouraging ownership of
homes, land, businesses, tools, and anything by which a person can create
wealth and which encourages citizens to think like owners. Laws that
discourage or undermine ownership are laws that undermine a society
of free and responsible citizens. Policy-makers must attend to the vital
role private property plays in developing and sustaining freedom. Home
ownership is a good start. Owners and renters think differently about the
places they inhabit. Home ownership can help foster virtues—such as
personal responsibility—necessary for healthy citizenship. Opportunities
for entrepreneurs must also be encouraged by laws friendly to start-ups.
Excessive regulations that create barriers to entry should be eliminated.
Worker-owned companies provide a creative and powerful avenue to
cultivating the habits of ownership. The particulars can vary from companies that are owned and controlled by the workers to programs that
give workers equity in the companies through Employee Stock Ownership Plans (ESOP).[3] The key is to provide opportunities for workers to
learn to think like owners and in the process to develop the habits and
virtues of ownership. When workers think of themselves also as owners, they bridge the gulf between labor and capital. The alienated worker,
described by Marx, who is separated from the final product of his labor
and divorced from any requirement to think beyond the narrow confines
of his particular task, is transformed into a worker who necessarily thinks
in terms of profits, losses, efficiency, and quality, and is incentivized to
creatively improve his performance as a means to increase the profitabil-
ity of the enterprise. Workers who think like owners will transform the
nature of a company, but they will also, in the process, develop virtues

3. For a good introduction to building a culture of ownership in a company see
Stack, *A Stake in the Outcome.*

and habits conducive to healthy democratic citizenship. Perhaps it goes without saying that the state should not take an active role in directly requiring companies to adopt operating procedures that turn workers into owners. The violation of property rights required by such a program would do more harm than good. However, federal and state governments can employ what Jefferson and Madison referred to as the "silent" operations of government, namely, incentives rooted in the tax policy to help encourage the expansion of a worker-owner class.

Third, scale matters. When policy-makers consider ways of encouraging property ownership, they must also attend to the fact that stewardship and scale are intimately joined. Stewardship turns on love: love for the thing stewarded, for past generations who provided the gift, and for future persons. But our capacity to love is finite. We can love best those things we know best; thus, our ability to know our private property is limited as well. Human-scale property is best suited to good stewardship. Thus, where possible, policy-makers should encourage the ownership of small properties and discourage the constant tendency of property to consolidate.

This final point merits a bit more discussion. First, if scale matters, then the state must employ its power to break up monopolies. Any corporation that controls more than a certain percentage of the market (the exact percentage will be a matter of discussion and judgment) should be broken up. Any corporation that exerts undue control over American citizens should be broken up. In this light, companies such as Amazon, BlackRock, Google, and Facebook must be broken into smaller competitive units that no longer hold monopolistic power. Of course, this remedy will elicit a strong and compelling objection: Breaking up monopolies will require a strong state, and the very process of eliminating monopolies will have the effect of making the state even stronger as it eliminates non-state centers of power. The reply indicates the delicate nature of this enterprise, for breaking up monopolies will only work if the welfare state is simultaneously reduced. This is, of course, no easy matter. However, as monopolies are broken, as economic power is decentralized, opportunities for property ownership will begin to emerge and expand. This expansion of opportunity will, ironically, have the effect of reducing the demand for welfare programs, for owners of productive property are better equipped for independence than those bereft of property.

Second, every society that aspires to be just must conduct a delicate dance between freedom and equality. As we have seen, the two ideals exist in creative tension: absolute freedom will eventually result in inequalities both social and material, and absolute equality, both social and material, cannot be achieved unless freedom is curtailed. However, in a democratic age, when citizens are constantly reminded of their equality, special care must be taken so that some sense of equality is in fact maintained. If a plausible account of equality disappears, citizens will be tempted to see "systemic" injustices, and conditions will be ripe for a revolution. This is precisely the situation that gives fuel to the Woke Socialists.

What can be done? First, it is important to recognize that there are more important aspects to equality than material equality. A just society must ensure that all citizens stand equally before the law. All must have equal access to the legal system. Wealth or poverty or race should not make a difference in the eyes of the courts. Guilt and innocence must turn on the facts of a case, not on the size of a person's bank account, status, or race. Second, all must be equal in terms of the ballot box. All votes should count the same regardless of the wealth of the voter. Third, opportunities to better oneself should ideally be equal, but in real terms this is only an ideal that can never be perfectly achieved. Opportunities depend on the community into which a person is born, the skills, commitment and resources of parents, as well as native intelligence, talent, and temperament. It is impossible to equalize all these factors, although things might be done on the margins to alleviate some of the most persistent and debilitating inequalities. Policy programs and private initiatives that provide education for disadvantaged persons and training for those who never learned the basic skills necessary to hold a job can help eliminate the most glaring inequalities. Ideally, these programs and initiatives should be rooted in local communities and be administered by individuals who know and love the communities they serve.

Socialists are, at least ostensibly, troubled by gross material inequalities. They claim that these are endemic to any capitalistic system, and because gross inequalities are unjust, capitalism is unjust. The problem, of course, is exacerbated by the rise of plutocracy, whereby the power of the state is harnessed by those with the means to buy access, and those without access (usually because they do not control sufficient wealth) are disadvantaged. When gross inequalities emerge in a democratic age—an age when equality is cherished as an ideal—it is natural for people to begin questioning the justice of the system. Thus, despite the protestations of some free-market fundamentalists, ignoring the ideal of equality is not possible or wise in a democratic age, nor is focusing exclusively on equality of opportunity sufficient. Recall that both Jefferson and Madison argued that some measures should be taken to lift citizens out of abject poverty and set them on the road to property ownership. Their commitment to freedom was tempered by the realization that if some citizens are indigent, they will be bad citizens, and the stability of the state would be jeopardized. Montesquieu, for his part, argued that extreme inequality was undesirable in a republic, for it is necessary that citizens identify with each other. They must conceive of themselves as playing the same game. They must not be so far removed from each other that all sense of connection is lost, and one way to unify citizens is to craft policies that expand the ownership of middle-class property. At the same time, Montesquieu recognized that pursuing extreme equality would necessarily destroy freedom. Thus, while anyone committed to fostering and preserving a free society will be loath to champion policies that advocate equality in an absolute sense, it is wise to support policies that eliminate the most extreme forms of inequality. A vibrant middle class must be the goal.

Centuries ago Plato argued that the "greatest of all injustices" is committed when citizens are allowed to sell all their possessions and then to remain in the city.[4] Presumably, no one sells all of his possessions unless he is under severe duress or has lost all concern for the future. Plato worried that these propertyless citizens would become drones, demanding services from the state while lacking the capacity to contribute to its health. If they did not become drones, they would become criminals. Plato's solution was the abolition of private property, at least for those in the leadership class and for soldiers tasked with protecting the city. In our nation today we should be just as concerned as Plato was about citizens who, for various reasons, find themselves bereft of property. We should be even more concerned when propertyless citizens express no desire to acquire property but, instead, clamor for services and economic security provided by the state.

This dynamic creates a fundamentally unstable social situation. Drones demanding services and security will, especially in a democratic society, fuel the expansion of the welfare state and sever the necessary connection between work and reward. Criminals, lacking any respect for the law, will show little regard for the institution of property. This will foster calls for an expanded police force and harsher penalties to rein in

4. Plato, *Republic*, 552b.

crime. The dissatisfied and propertyless masses will readily sympathize with those who argue that the system is fundamentally unjust and rigged to benefit some at the expense of everyone else. The abuses of police power will provide further reasons to condemn the system as a whole. Those without property will rage against those who possess it. They will destroy property as the emblem of systemic injustice, and they will readily succumb to utopian fantasies extolling the elimination of private property and promising a world of justice that will arise in the wake of the destruction. In the United States, the rhetoric of racial injustice has provided both fuel for the protests and an aura of moral legitimacy to the revolutionary enterprise.

America has often been called "the land of opportunity." Immigrants come to America to take advantage of the opportunities that freedom affords. The American Dream consists in finding success on the basis of hard work and determination. A crucial kind of equality exists if citizens all have a desire to own property and if the system is arranged so that anyone with determination and hard work can become a property owner. This is not equality of material goods or of outcomes. It is, as some put it, "equality of opportunity." But we must recognize that such equality depends on an underlying equality in the desire to own property. When that desire is lost among a significant segment of the populace, the result will be that some citizens are striving for property ownership while others are seeking consumer goods and government services. This division represents a clash of cultures. It represents two competing and incompatible ways of seeing the world. If those seeking government services and security come to represent a majority of voting citizens, some form of socialism will win, and our nation will be fundamentally changed. If, on the other hand, those animated by a desire to own property prevail, the American constitutional order may yet be preserved. The stakes are high, and the outcome is not at all certain.

This leads us to a surprising conclusion: those with property should actively support policies to alleviate the greatest inequalities for the sake of preserving our constitutional order. If extreme inequalities create the impression that the system is unjust and at the same time erode the aspiration to own property among some citizens, then, in the name of maintaining our freedom, those with property must recognize a duty to those without. In aristocratic ages the duty of the nobility was understood. Nobility brought with it obligations: *noblesse oblige*. Today we need to recognize a new form of this obligation but reformulated for a democratic age: *proprietas oblige*, the obligation of property ownership.[5] Those with capital have the obligation to work toward a broader distribution of capital rather than, as is so often the case, toward the expansion of government services. This, on its face, is counter-intuitive. Isn't it more reasonable to expect that those with capital will work to expand their own holdings rather than the holdings of others? To answer this question we can appeal to enlightened self-interest. As property ownership becomes increasingly consolidated, as the number of citizens who own property, or who aspire to own property, declines, the newly formed proletarian majority will eventually attack private property through the ballot box. Enlightened self-interest will lead a holder of property to become a champion of the broad ownership of property. The principle is clear: if you have property and if you want to help preserve the social and political conditions necessary for its preservation, work to promote policies that expand property ownership. This is true even if it means that your own holdings are not as large as they could be if their expansion were your sole concern. Here we see a tangible connection between property, citizenship, and the common good.

Socialists condemn capitalism because it fosters inequality. However, at least some of the inequalities that the socialists find so offensive are the result, not of the free market, but of the incestuous relationship between the market and the state. Cronyism should be an affront to us all. Furthermore, one must never forget that excursions into socialism in the twentieth century did not result in the elimination of inequalities. The state never withered away as Marx predicted. The dictatorship of the proletariat never materialized. Those who controlled the levers of power also controlled access to the trough of state goods and services. Rather than distribute those goods and services equitably, this new plutocratic class used power and access to enrich themselves and their cronies. It turned out that Orwell was right: in the world of socialism, all animals may be equal, but some are more equal than others.

Yet hope springs eternal. The siren song of utopia is ever present. The dream is as old as Plato and as fresh as today's newsfeed, but it is as elusive as ever. It is also as seductive as ever, and an entire generation is being tempted by promises of endless services from the hand of a caring state.

5. Röpke makes a similar point when he insists that "richesse oblige," although his focus is not specifically on property, *per se*, but rather on wealth more generally. See *A Humane Economy*, 132.

The Achievement of Freedom

We are creatures of habit. It is easy to become accustomed to the status quo. Specifically, it is easy to come to believe that our political freedoms are the product of natural forces, that democratic freedom is the inevitable result of an historical process. Freedom, we are told, is the natural condition of human beings in a state of nature, and political freedom is merely the extension of that natural state of affairs. Or alternatively, we are told that history is moving toward freedom or that freedom will spontaneously blossom if impediments are removed. Nothing could be further from the truth. As we have seen, political freedom is a remarkable achievement. The American Founders did not invent political freedom nor did they perfect it. When they declared their independence from Great Britain and set out to establish a new nation, they did not begin with a blank slate and a set of abstract ideas. Instead, they built on what they had inherited from centuries of experimentation and examples, good and bad, stretching back into antiquity. They understood that building a free society is no simple enterprise. They carefully borrowed and arranged principles and practices long tried and tested. Their knowledge of history and firsthand experience in the self-government of the colonies were indispensable. Furthermore, they had lived under the threat of tyranny for long enough that they had an acute taste for freedom, but they also clearly grasped the difficulty of achieving it.

They handed us a constitutional order that could not survive apart from the virtue of citizens. They understood that political self-government requires government of one's own appetites and desires. They understood that virtue was the only way that citizens could hope to approximate this internal check on appetites that constantly threaten to break out into chaos and anarchy. And they understood that this constitutional order they built was only suited to a middle-class people, citizens who, by and large, were careful owners of their property, citizens who aspired to independence from the encroaching power of the state, regardless of its seemingly benevolent intentions. They understood that power always tends toward consolidation and that the best way to thwart that consolidation is to keep power—both political and economic—diffuse.

Perhaps the matter can be expressed this way: maintaining freedom is important. But this can only be achieved if we diligently maintain the *conditions* in which freedom flourishes. For some time these conditions have been eroding through inattention born of complacency, and they have been actively undermined by those with a social and political vision that runs counter to that of the Founders. The Woke Socialists dream of a world of perfect equality, social justice, and stable weather. Putting matters in such a light reveals the utopian impulse at the heart of their project. Equality is a good ideal, but it must be tempered by freedom. A society of free citizens will always have some degree of inequality. A wise statesman will be able to balance these competing ideals. Justice is a noble ideal, but the term has been twisted into a shorthand for social aspirations that pit the grievances of a variety of identity groups against the "systemic" and often invisible abuses of the white, male patriarchy—a group to which the Founders belonged and which immediately calls into question their wisdom and their work. This has led some to wonder if the Constitution is outdated and in need of a serious overhaul or even a replacement. When these concerns are accompanied by the frantic hand-wringing of "climate" hysteria, the political prudence that would govern the studied and gradual improvement of what we have inherited is replaced by a militant call to overturn the system in the name of saving the world.

Rather than seeing a strong and vibrant middle class rooted in private property as an indispensable bulwark supporting political freedom, these twenty-first-century Jacobins see private property as a feature of an unjust capitalist system that must be replaced. When that glorious day arrives, equality and justice will prevail and the weather will behave as we demand. Of course, perfect equality and justice will never be achieved, nor will the climate submit to our wishes. This means that the Woke Socialists will be perpetually frustrated but, in their optimistic fever dreams, remain forever energized to strive with all the fervor they can muster and all the political power they can seize to create the elusive world that remains just beyond their grasp or at least just beyond the next election.

Hovering over the revolutionary frenzy of Woke Socialism is the plutocratic class desperately intent on maintaining its power and quite willing to do whatever is necessary to do so. This dynamic and perverse relationship is characterized by two groups who are joined by their disdain of middle-class citizens characterized by middle-class virtues and private property.

There are, ultimately, goods beyond private property. These goods include personal virtue, strong communities, and political freedom. Private property, however, is an important means by which these goods can be preserved and enhanced. Strong families with productive property upon which they work provide a crucial buffer against the natural—and justifiable—tendencies of a proletarianized society where propertyless citizens express their insecurity by demanding services from the state. Since political freedom is not natural, it must be cultivated—the gardening metaphor should not go unnoticed. Stewardship of freedom means carefully and lovingly cultivating and stewarding private property. But the fact of private property cannot be realized apart from a culture that fosters a desire to own it. This is the crux of the matter. Our constitutional system depends on a culture of free and responsible citizens who own property or aspire to do so. If we fail to maintain (or revive) a culture of private property, our constitutional order will prove itself to be antiquated, just as the Woke Socialists contend. The alternatives are clear. The revolutionary momentum is picking up speed. There is much work to be done. Defenders of private property are needed. But even more, we need mature citizens committed to the hard work of stewarding private property and, in the process, stewarding our republic.

Afterword

Building a Multiracial
Middle-Class Coalition

> All worthy things that are in peril as the world now stands,
> those are my care. And for my part, I shall not wholly fail of my
> task, though Gondor should perish, if anything passes through
> this night that can still grow fair or bear fruit and flower again
> in days to come. For I also am a steward.
>
> —J.R.R. TOLKIEN, *THE RETURN OF THE KING*

IN THE SPRING OF 2020 an initiative from The World Economic Forum was rolled out to the world. They called it the Great Reset. The worldwide coronavirus pandemic provided a focal point and a sense of urgency. The looming "existential threat" of climate change made sweeping action absolutely necessary in order to prevent a catastrophe that would dwarf the carnage inflicted by the coronavirus. The killing of George Floyd in May touched off protests in the U.S. and around the globe raising awareness of racial injustice that seemed to require profound systemic changes. The common denominator: crisis. The common agent of change? Government power in partnership with many of the world's largest multinational corporations. According to the WEF website, "The world must act jointly and swiftly to revamp all aspects of our societies and economies, from education to social contracts and working conditions. Every country, from the United States to China, must participate, and every industry, from oil and gas to tech, must be transformed. In short, we need a "Great Reset" of capitalism."[1]

The plan to "revamp all aspects of our societies and economies" represents a sweeping vision for world-wide transformation that mirrors, on a larger scale, the U.S.-focused vision of the Green New Deal. The collaboration of national governments, international organizations, and transnational corporations suggests a consolidation of power unlike any other peace-time initiative in history. If every country "from the United States to China" joins forces with the world's most powerful corporations, the ability to effect change will be almost irresistible. Consider, in this context, some of the "partner" corporations listed at the WEF website: Amazon, Apple, Barclays, BlackRock, Boing, China Construction Bank, Deutsche Bank, Discovery, European Investment Bank, Facebook, Goldman Sachs, IBM, JPMorgan Chase & Co., Kaiser Permanente, LinkedIn, Mastercard, Microsoft, Nasdaq, Netflix, The New York Times, PayPal, Pfizer, Tyson Foods, UPS, Visa, Walmart, Western Union, and dozens more.[2] What is described here is a global plutocracy.

It's not hard to imagine that an America First president like Donald Trump would object to the globalist vision of the Great Reset. However, Joe Biden enthusiastically embraced this agenda. Indeed, in November of 2020, soon after the election, former Secretary of State John Kerry, recently tapped to be Biden's "Climate Tsar," participated in a panel discussion hosted by The World Economic Forum addressing the Great Reset.[3] Kerry was asked if he thought the United States would go along. Kerry was emphatic. "Yes, it [the Great Reset] will happen.... And I think it will happen with greater speed and with greater intensity than a lot of people might imagine.[4]

What will this Great Reset entail? It's hard to anticipate all the directions and implications, but those who are pushing it provide some hints. A central feature of this brave new world is the end of private property. In a short WEF video, titled "8 Predictions for the World in 2030," the first prediction shows the smiling face of a young man with the seemingly innocuous (or ominous) caption: "You'll own nothing. And you'll

1. Schwab, *World Economic Forum*, June 3, 2020.

2. *World Economic Forum*, "Our Partners."

3. De Caro, *World Economic Forum*, Nov. 17, 2020.

4. Haskins, *The Hill*, Dec. 3, 2020.

be happy."[5] In a related article that lays out more details, we're told that by 2030 "all products will have become services."[6] A Danish MP named Ida Auken imagines this utopian future: "I don't own anything. I don't own a car. I don't own a house. I don't own any appliances or any clothes."[7]

The goal of the Great Reset is to combat climate change, eliminate inequality, and establish government and corporate structures that can achieve those goals while creating buffers against future global crises, including pandemics. In this scheme the sovereignty of individual nations will necessarily diminish, and international organizations will increase in scope and power. The energy and organizational capabilities of multinational corporations will provide a natural complement to the transnational political organizations. Both the nation-state and private property will come to be seen as antiquated remnants of a fundamentally unjust system characterized by capitalism, inequality, racism, sexism, and an array of phobias including homophobia, transphobia, and xenophobia. The concentration of political, economic, and social power represented by the combination of Global Plutocracy and Woke Socialism will make resistance to this all-encompassing program virtually impossible.

Clearly, this Reset represents a political, economic, and social vision that is radically different from the one imagined by the American Founders (and remarkably similar to the Green New Deal). If the Great Reset or the Green New Deal (or something similar) is ever implemented, the casualty will be our constitutional order. The essential connection between political liberty and private property is denied by these wide-eyed planners, who dream of a world of perfect freedom, perfect equality, perfect justice, and perfect weather. However, if the arguments laid out in this book are correct, the actual result of their sweeping political and economic annexations will be the loss of freedom, abject equality for the masses but privilege for the plutocrats and their technocratic lackeys, and the proliferation of arbitrary injustices propagated by state and corporate leaders. And to top it all off, the weather will still be capricious.

What, then is the alternative? The only option that offers a clear path to preserving our inherited constitutional order is the construction of a multiracial middle-class coalition that resists the utopian siren song of political, social, and economic revolution. Given the agenda being pushed

5. World Economic Forum, "You'll Own Nothing and You'll be Happy."

6. Parker, *World Economic Forum*, Nov. 12, 2016.

7. Auken, *World Economic Forum*, Nov. 11, 2016.

by leaders on the Left, if an alternative coalition is to be built, it will have to begin with those moderates, conservatives, and disaffected refugees from the Left who have not been co-opted by the plutocracy or become content with servility. The result will not be recognizably Republican or Democratic as measured by current standards. However, building this coalition will not be simple. Democrats have long presented themselves as the party of the working man and accused Republicans of being the party of the wealthy: Main Street vs. Wall Street. This duality would seem to be born out in the 2020 presidential campaign where a New York billionaire was replaced by a man of humble roots who for years proudly rode the train and was referred to as "lunch-bucket Joe." However, looks can be deceiving, and narratives, if repeated often enough, can seem true even when they are patently false. Joe Biden in particular, and the Democratic Party in general, has carefully cultivated the political gestures and rhetoric suggesting identification and concern with the working class and the poor while at the same time pandering to the wishes of Wall Street, especially Big Tech, which controls information and thus significantly influences the outcomes of elections. Democrats have long taken for granted the votes of minority Americans while promising policies to help alleviate poverty and social breakdown. In reality, the policies have created a permanent underclass which, in political terms, has created generational clients of the Democratic Party. This is beginning to change.[8] Part of the change was the disruption caused by Donald Trump's unconventional candidacy and presidency. Many of his policies were aimed at helping American workers, protecting American jobs, and returning manufacturing to America. In a curious twist, a billionaire hotelier from New York was able to connect with many working-class Americans, and while he lost a close election in 2020, he garnered surprisingly strong support from blacks and Latinos.[9] This small success in the context of a lost campaign suggests the necessary starting point.

Any serious multiracial coalition must address the issue of race head-on. Ignoring racial issues will not make them dissipate. It will only provide an opportunity for the race radicals to control the narrative. Black Lives Matter is a perfect example. Rather than ignoring BLM and hoping it will burn out or go away, serious people must confront it directly, expose it for what it is, and provide an alternative that takes

8. See, for instance, Blexit. https://blexitfoundation.org/
9. Caldwell, *The New York Post*, Nov. 7, 2020.

seriously the challenges besetting the black community while attending simultaneously to the challenges facing the poor and working class of all ethnicities.

Black Lives Matter and other revolutionary groups have gained significant rhetorical and political advantage by claiming that racism is "systemic."[10] They insist that racism is, as we're told by *The New York Times'* "1619 Project," at the root of "nearly everything that has truly made America exceptional." In other words, all of American social, cultural, economic, and political systems are racist to the core.[11] If that is the case, then those who aspire to live in a color-blind society are fooling themselves and are deeply, though perhaps unknowingly, entwined in racist structures. They are racists and don't even know it. They have benefited from racist "systems" and therefore are guilty. They must be punished and re-educated. Racist systems must be destroyed. The rhetoric of "systemic" racism makes race guilt unavoidable and revolution increasingly possible. But race guilt is antithetical to reconciliation, peace, or justice. It provides a rhetorical cudgel with which to dominate opponents, and revolution is the means to destroy the current order and usher in a Marxist-utopian paradise.

Ibram X. Kendi makes a similar rhetorical move. In his best-selling book, *How to be an Antiracist*, Kendi asserts that one can be either an antiracist—and thereby fall in line with his radical racist agenda—or one is de facto a racist who must be countered. "There is no neutrality in the racism struggle. The opposite of 'racist' isn't 'not racist.' It is 'antiracist'.... The claim of 'not racist' neutrality is a mask for racism."[12] According to Kendi, there is no middle ground, and any aspiration to transcend race is simply a ploy of white supremists intent on maintaining power.

To be clear, we must take seriously the painful history of race in America while at the same time refusing to allow BLM and other race-grievance opportunists to shape the narrative. An example of this narrative-shaping power came in the wake of the death of George Floyd in May of 2020. Floyd's death unleashed a wave of protests, ostensibly provoked by anger at systemic racial injustice and exemplified by police brutality toward unarmed black men. Many of these "mostly peaceful" protests,

10. See for instance the display titled "Whiteness" at the Smithsonian Institution Museum of African American History and Culture.

11. Silverstein, "The 1619 Project: Introduction," *The New York Times Magazine,* Aug. 18, 2019, pg. 4.

12. Kendi, *How to be an Antiracist,* 9.

as the media generally described them, led to violence and widespread destruction of private property.

We must ask a serious and perhaps disconcerting question: was race really the central issue motivating the protests and violence? Are white Americans simply incapable of recognizing their deep-seated racial prejudices? That's what Black Lives Matter and its progressive supporters, black and white, claim. Of course, racist individuals exist, and they always will. But most Americans are not racists. Most Americans are far less concerned about race than they are about providing for their families and living at peace with their neighbors. Something other than racism drove these protests, even as racist rhetoric was widely employed to both explain and justify them.

Here's a thought experiment: would the riots have occurred if America were overwhelmingly a middle-class, property-owning society? What if persistent, generational poverty and the hopelessness created by broken families and failed social welfare policies disappeared tomorrow and were replaced by propertied citizens possessing middle-class virtues such as self-control, independence, thrift, concern for the future, and neighborliness?

The profound suffering and despair of the American underclass is being manipulated by self-righteous grievance professionals actively working to subvert the ideals upon which our nation was built. They are using race as a weapon in a war to gain personal advantages and to transform the United States, and they are willing to engage in intimidation, violence, and property destruction to achieve their ends. They scorn middle-class Americans who work hard, acquire property, and care for it.

We do well to ask why private property is so often the target both in the theoretical blueprints for revolution as well as the concrete destruction on the street. The answer is that in attacking private property, the revolutionaries are striking at one of the bedrock institutions of a free society and a tangible impediment to the success of the revolution. Private property must be demonized and destroyed, for as long as citizens own private property, as long as some individuals enjoy the independence made possible by the ownership of capital, the revolutionaries are confronted with a powerful obstacle. The sight of free men and women—of all races and ethnicities—exercising their freedom over their own property represents a constant reminder that a noble alternative exists to the false hopes offered by the purveyors of a socialist utopia. Private property and those who understand the duty of stewardship are the natural and eternal enemies of the revolutionaries represented by the Green New Deal, the Great Reset, and Black Lives Matter.

The American republic, as I have argued at length, was designed for a propertied citizenry; the ownership of property cultivates the independence necessary for self-government. Consider the words of Thomas Jefferson, from an 1814 letter describing American society to a British correspondent: "We have no Paupers. . . . Most of the laboring class possess property, cultivate their own lands, have families, and from the demand for their labor are enabled to exact from the rich and the competent such prices as enable them to be fed abundantly, clothed above mere decency, to labor moderately and raise their families."[13] This is a good ideal toward which a renewed vision of political freedom must aspire but refashioned to fit twenty-first-century realities.

Alexis de Tocqueville noted that the battles over property and property rights so common in Europe were unheard of in America, which he attributed to the vast majority of Americans being property owners. Tocqueville noted that revolutions threaten property; thus, societies where property is broadly owned are naturally inoculated against revolutionary energies. Widely distributed property, according to Tocqueville, helps to cultivate a respect for the property of others, and this spills over into respect for the rights of others more broadly. A propertied citizenry is not given to rioting, revolution, or the wanton destruction of property.[14] The broad ownership of private property is a natural impediment to revolutionary fervor.

One of the challenges that will confront a new middle-class coalition is inducing citizens to aspire to become owners of property. Our society has already traveled far down the revolutionary road. Many Americans don't own property. But more troubling than that, many Americans have no desire to become owners of property. They are seemingly content with the services provided by the caring state while at the same time easily manipulated by the purveyors of revolutionary policies that, if successful, promise to unleash an unlimited flood of goods and services while fundamentally transforming the nation. It's a childhood fantasy transformed into a political program.

Poor blacks and other minorities know that something is amiss, but the problem is not systemic racism. It is systemic poverty and

13. Jefferson, Letter to Thomas Cooper, September 10, 1814.

14. Tocqueville, *Democracy in America*, 608–10.

demoralization brought about by a complex array of social and politi-cal forces that affect poor whites and Latinos as well as blacks: broken families, especially absentee fathers; the declining influence of churches; schools that fail to educate and an anti-education culture; welfare policies that create dependence and undermine an ethic of work indispensable for entry into the middle class; and regulations and cronyism that create barriers to entry and reward gigantic corporations at the expense of small businesses and entrepreneurs. It's not hard to see how groups like BLM could manipulate these facts to create a narrative of systemic oppression in which blacks, along with white progressives, join forces to burn the system down.

America must strengthen its middle class; it must also mark out a clear path for the poor to reach the middle class, though the obstacles here are complex. They include social pathologies that can be solved only by individuals and communities committed to personal responsibility, stable families, education, and hard work. In addition, failed policies ostensibly aimed at helping the poor have instead reduced them to a permanent—and understandably resentful—underclass. Despair mixed with shame and fueled by a pernicious ideology of racial resentment en-ergizes Woke Socialism and leads to chaos in the streets.

A new middle-class coalition must highlight the necessary connec-tion between work and reward. Rather than succumbing to the social justice agenda, with its limitless demands for free goods and services paid for by the labor of others, political leaders must focus their atten-tion on the poor and marginalized—the people Christ called "the least of these"—by providing opportunities for 1) meaningful work and 2) the ownership of productive property. When economic reward follows hard work, the social and moral benefits are incalculable. Any economic struc-tures or public policies that undermine the connection between work and reward or obstruct the possibility of acquiring private property must be eliminated. Every effort must be made to ensure that ownership is a viable, desirable, and attainable reality. In short, black property matters.

The challenges America faces are complex. Many of the social pa-thologies we confront today are intertwined with political and economic arrangements that actively cause harm rather than health. The ownership of property can, as I have argued, provide a vital catalyst for the rein-vigoration of the American republic. Property ownership can call forth virtues that are necessary for political freedom and healthy citizenship. Property ownership can provide a means by which families can support themselves, around which healthy communities can grow, and through which the practice of neighborliness can emerge. When we come to see ourselves as part of an intact community passing through time, we will be better disposed to see ourselves as stewards tasked with the responsibility to care for our property, our cultural inheritance, the natural world, and each other. In the process, we will be better equipped to see that each person, created in God's image, is valuable beyond price.

The hour is late. The forces arrayed against private property, political freedom, and human dignity are gathering strength. They have been laying plans and preparing the ground for decades. There is no guarantee of success. However, there is still hope. A multiracial middle-class coalition is needed, led by clear-sighted individuals who understand what is at stake, who can articulate a viable and attractive alternative to utopia's seductive call, and who have the courage to act.

Acknowledgements

THIS BOOK HAS BEEN in process for a long time. Some of the background work was completed with the assistance of a grant from the late Earhart Foundation. I continue to be grateful to that organization for its generosity over the years. Various people aided this project in various ways. While those named here are not responsible for the final product, I am grateful for the advice, insight, and direction offered along the way. Thanks to Jeremy Beer, John Ehrett, Ethan Foster, Daniel Kishi, Daniel J. Mahoney, Derrick Max, Joshua Mitchell, Jason Peters, Jeff Polet, Howard Schmidt, and Reagan Van Belle. Thanks also to Gayle Reinhardt, Vickie Thornhill, and Pierce Gillen for research and editing help at various stages of this project. Finally, I am grateful to the production team at Wipf & Stock for their professionalism.

Bibliography

Adams, John to Abigail Adams, Oct. 29, 1775. https://www.gutenberg.org/files/34123/34123-h/34123-h.htm.

Adams, John to James Sullivan, May 26, 1776. https://founders.archives.gov/documents/Adams/06-04-02-0091.

AOC Countdown Clock. http://aoc-clock.com/.

Aquinas, Thomas, *Summa Theologica*, excerpted in Aquinas, *On Law, Morality, and Politics*, 2nd edition, trans. Richard J. Regan (Indianapolis: Hackett, 2002).

Aristotle, *The Complete Works of Aristotle*, ed. Richard McKeon. *Nicomachean Ethics* trans. W.D. Ross; *Politics* trans. Benjamin Jowett (New York: The Modern Library, 2001).

Augustine, *City of God*. Translated by Marus Dods (New York: The Modern Library, 1993).

Auken, Ida, "Here's How Life Could Change in My City by the Year 2030," *World Economic Forum*, Nov. 11, 2016. https://www.weforum.org/agenda/2016/11/how-life-could-change-2030/.

Belloc, Hilaire, *The Servile State* (Indianapolis: The Liberty Fund, Inc., 1977).

Blake, Aaron, "More Young People Voted for Bernie Sanders than Trump and Clinton Combined—By a Lot," The Washington Post, June 20, 2016. https://www.washingtonpost.com/news/the-fix/wp/2016/06/20/more-young-people-voted-for-bernie-sanders-than-trump-and-clinton-combined-by-a-lot/.

Blexit. https://blexitfoundation.org/.

Broady, Kristin E., Edelberg, Wendy, and Moss, Emily, "An Eviction Moratorium without Rental Assistance Hurts Smaller Landlords, Too," *The Hamilton Project*, Sept. 21, 2020.

https://www.hamiltonproject.org/blog/an_eviction_moratorium_without_rental_assistance_hurts_smaller_landlords_too.

Burke, Edmund, *Reflections on the Revolution in France* (Indianapolis: Liberty Fund, 1999).

Caldwell, Gianno, "Why the Supposedly Racist Trump Grew His Numbers with Black and Latino Voters," *The New York Post*, Nov. 7, 2020. https://nypost.com/2020/11/07/why-trump-grew-his-numbers-with-black-and-latino-voters/.

Carey, George W. and McClellan, James, ed. *The Federalist Papers* (Indianapolis: Liberty Fund, 2001).

Carmel, Margaret, "City of Boise Set to Use Facial Recognition in City Hall and City Hall West," *Idaho Press*, July 6, 2019. https://www.idahopress.com/news/local/

city-of-boise-set-to-use-facial-recognition-in-city/article_9c1d4b72-daf3–53c9–8597-c4f2c296197b.html.

Chesterton, G.K., *The Outline of Sanity* (Norfolk, VA: IHS Press, 2002).

Collins, Victoria, "Covid-19 and Universal Basic Income: Lessons for Governments from the Tech World," *Forbes*, March 19, 2020. https://www.forbes.com/sites/victoriacollins/2020/03/19/covid-19-and-universal-basic-income-lessons-for-governments-from-the-tech-world/?sh=605964ea57ec.

De Caro, Beatrice, "The Great Reset: Building Future Resilience to Global Risks," *World Economic Forum*, Nov. 17, 2020. https://www.weforum.org/agenda/2020/11/the-great-reset-building-future-resilience-to-global-risks.

Democratic Socialists of America. "What is Democratic Socialism?" https://www.dsausa.org/about-us/what-is-democratic-socialism/#govt.

Earle, Ethan, "A Brief History of Occupy," *Rosa Luxemburg Stifung*, Nov. 25, 2012. https://rosalux.nyc/a-history-of-occupy/

Edwards, John, *CBS News*, July 28, 2004. https://www.cbsnews.com/news/text-of-john-edwards-speech/.

Fitz-Gibbon, Jorge, "Black Lives Matter Organizer Calls Chicago Looting 'Reparation,'" *The New York Post*, Aug. 11, 2020. https://nypost.com/2020/08/11/black-lives-matter-organizer-calls-chicago-looting-reparation/.

French Republic Constitution of 1793. https://oll.libertyfund.org/pages/1793-french-republic-constitution-of-1793.

Frizell, Sam, "Bernie Sanders Advisor Explains the Campaign's Ad Strategy," *Time*, June 15, 2016. https://time.com/4370312/bernie-sanders-advisor-explains-the-campaigns-ad-strategy/

Frohnen, Bruce, ed., *The American Republic: Primary Sources*, (Indianapolis: Liberty Fund, 2002).

Galsworthy, John, "Quality," 1911. http://www.gutenberg.org/files/4261/4261-h/4261-h.htm#link2H_4_0012.

Gates, Jr., Henry Louis, "The Truth Behind '40 Acres and a Mule," *PBS*. https://www.pbs.org/wnet/african-americans-many-rivers-to-cross/history/the-truth-behind-40-acres-and-a-mule/.

Gorby, Pascal-Emmanuel, "A Science-Based Case for Ending the Porn Epidemic," *American Greatness*, December 15, 2019. https://amgreatness.com/2019/12/15/a-science-based-case-for-ending-the-porn-epidemic/.

Hannah-Jones, Nikole et al., "The 1619 Project," *The New York Times*, August 18, 2019.

Haskins, Justin, "John Kerry Reveals Biden's Devotion to Radical 'Great Reset' Movement," *The Hill*, Dec. 3, 2020. https://www.msn.com/en-us/news/politics/john-kerry-reveals-bidens-devotion-to-radical-great-reset-movement/ar-BB1bBu34.

Hayek, F.A., *The Road to Serfdom* (Chicago: The University of Chicago Press, 1994).

Herndon, Astead W., "Alexandra Ocasio-Cortez Has Never Spoken to Joe Biden. Here's What She Would Say," *The New York Times*, April 13, 2020. https://www.nytimes.com/2020/04/13/us/politics/aoc-progressives-joe-biden.html.

Hess, Abigail, "Elizabeth Warren's $1.25 Trillion Education Plan Aims to End the Cycle of Student Debt—Here's How," *CNBC*, April 23, 2019. https://www.cnbc.com/2019/04/23/elizabeth-warren-proposes-free-college-and-eliminating-student-debt.html.

Homer, *Iliad*. Translated by Robert Fitzgerald (New York: Farar, Straus & Giroux, 2004).

Horowitz, Juliana Menasce, Igielnik, Ruth, and Kochhar, Rakesh, "Trends in Income and Wealth Inequality," *Pew Research Center*, January 9, 2020. https://www.pewresearch.org/social-trends/2020/01/09/trends-in-income-and-wealth-inequality/.

Hyneman, Charles S. and Lutz, Donald ed., *American Political Writings During the Founding Era 1760–1805*, ed. (Indianapolis: Liberty Fund, 1983).

Jefferson, Thomas, Letter to Thomas Cooper, September 10, 1814. https://founders.archives.gov/documents/Jefferson/03–07–02–0471.

Jefferson, Thomas, *The Works of Thomas Jefferson*, vol. VIII, ed. Paul Leicester Ford (New York: G.P. Putnam's Sons, 1904).

Kavanaugh, J., concurring in Alabama Association of Realtors v. Department of Health and Human Services, June 29, 2021.

Kendi, Ibram X., *How to be an Antiracist* (New York: One World, 2019).

Keynes, John Maynard, "Economic Possibilities for Our Grandchildren," 1930. http://www.econ.yale.edu/smith/econ116a/keynes1.pdf.

Khalid, Amrita, "Elizabeth Warren Hopes Policy Will Set Her Apart in 2020," *Daily Dot*, April 22, 2019. https://www.dailydot.com/layer8/elizabeth-warren-2020-platform-policies/.

Kirchgaessner, Stephanie, "Warren Attacks CEOs Who 'Wrecked' Economy," *Financial Times*, Sept. 6, 2012. https://web.archive.org/web/20120908033052/http://www.ft.com/cms/s/0/5718c926-f7d4–11e1-ba54–00144feabdco.html#axzz5s4IqiW8I.

Knight Foundation, "Free Expression on Campus: What College Students Think About First Amendment Issues," *Knight Foundation*, March 12, 2018. https://knightfoundation.org/reports/free-expression-on-campus-what-college-students-think-about-first-amendment-issues/.

Koch, Charles G., "This is the One Issue Where Bernie Sanders is Right." *The Washington Post*, Feb. 18, 2016. http://wapo.st/1Tpei9f?tid=ss_mail&utm_term=.81321369a6f0.

Kopf, Dan, "What's a Universal Basic Income Doing in Ocasio-Cortez's "Green New Deal"?, Quartz, Dec. 13, 2018. https://qz.com/1493569/whats-a-universal-basic-income-doing-in-ocasio-cortezs-green-new-deal/.

Kotkin, Joel, "America's Drift Toward Feudalism," *The Journal of American Affairs*, November 20, 2019.

——— *The Coming of Neo-Feudalism: A Warning to the Global Middle Class* (New York: Encounter Books, 2020).

Kristof, Nicholas, "The Children of Pornhub," *The New York Times*, Dec. 4, 2020. https://www.nytimes.com/2020/12/04/opinion/sunday/pornhub-rape-trafficking.html.

Levin, Sam, "Movement to Defund Police Gains 'Unprecedented' Support Across US," *The Guardian*, June 4, 2020. https://www.theguardian.com/us-news/2020/jun/04/defund-the-police-us-george-floyd-budgets.

Locke, John, *Two Treatises of Government*, ed. Peter Laslett (New York: Cambridge University Press, 1960).

Madison, James, *The Writings of James Madison*, vol. 6, ed. Gaillard Hunt (New York: G.P. Putnam's Sons, 1906).

Marx, Karl, *The Marx-Engels Reader*, ed. Robert C. Tucker, 2nd edition (New York: Norton, 1978).

Mason, Paul, "My Manifesto for a Post-Carbon Future," New Statesman, July 17, 2019. https://www.newstatesman.com/politics/environment/2019/07/my-manifesto-post-carbon-future.

Matamoros, Elizabeth, "Sanders: Rethinking How Society Functions Could be the 'Silver Lining' to Pandemic," *The Washington Free Beacon*, May 17, 2020. https://freebeacon.com/politics/sanders-rethinking-how-society-functions-could-be-silver-lining-to-pandemic/.

Mises, Ludwig von, *Socialism*, trans. J. Kahane (New Haven, CT: Yale University Press, 1951).

Montesquieu, *The Spirit of the Laws*, ed. by Anne M. Cohler, Basis C. Miller, and Harold S. Stone (New York: Cambridge University Press, 1989).

Nash, George H., *Books and the Founding Fathers* (Louisville, KY: Butler Books, 2007).

Ocasio-Cortez, Alexandria, "The Green New Deal Fact Sheet and FAQ," *The Heartland Institute*, Feb. 8, 2019. https://www.heartland.org/publications-resources/publications/green-new-deal-fact-sheet-and-faq-from-rep-alexandria-ocasio-cortez-and-sen-edward-markey.

Onepoll, "Covid-19 Has Changed Americans' Opinions on Universal Health Care," *Onepoll*, May 18, 2020. https://www.onepoll.us/covid-19-has-changed-americans-opinions-on-universal-health-care/.

Osterweil, Vicky, *In Defense of Looting* (Bold Type Books, 2020).

Parker, Ceri, "8 Predictions for the World in 2030," *World Economic Forum*, Nov. 12, 2016. https://www.weforum.org/agenda/2016/11/8-predictions-for-the-world-in-2030/?utm_content=bufferdda7f&utm_medium=social&utm_source=facebook.com&utm_campaign=buffer.

Pasley, James, "I Documented Every Surveillance Camera on My Way to Work in New York City, and it Revealed a Dystopian Reality," *Business Insider*, Dec. 6, 2019. https://www.businessinsider.com/how-many-security-cameras-in-new-york-city-2019–12?op=1#when-my-editor-assigned-this-i-agreed-immediately-it-was-only-as-i-went-home-that-day-noticing-all-the-cameras-around-me-that-i-began-to-realize-the-truth-behind-the-saying-ignorance-is-bliss-1.

Penn, William, *The Political Writings of William Penn* (Indianapolis: Liberty Fund, 2002).

Pew Research Center, "The American Middle Class is Losing Ground," Dec. 9, 2015. https://www.pewsocialtrends.org/2015/12/09/the-american-middle-class-is-losing-ground/.

Pipes, Richard, *Property and Freedom* (New York: Vintage, 1999).

Plato. *Laws*. Translated by Treavor J. Saunders (New York: Penguin, 1970).

———— *Republic*. Translated by C.D.C. Reeve (Indianapolis: Hackett, 2004).

Rasmussen Report, "31% Think U.S. Civil War Likely Soon," June 27, 2018. https://www.rasmussenreports.com/public_content/politics/general_politics/june_2018/31_think_u_s_civil_war_likely_soon."

Röpke, Wilhelm, *A Humane Economy* (Wilmington: ISI Books, 1998).

———— *The Moral Foundations of Civil Society* (New Brunswick: Transaction, 2002).

Rousseau, Jean Jacques, *The Basic Political Writings*, 2nd edition, translated and edited by Donald A. Cress (Indianapolis: Hackett, 2011).

———— *The Confessions of Jean Jacques Rousseau*, vol. 1 (London: Privately Printed for the Members of the Aldus Society, 1903).

Sanders, Bernie "Wall Street and Economy Speech," *Market Watch*, Jan. 5, 2016. https://www.marketwatch.com/story/text-of-bernie-sanders-wall-street-and-economy-speech-2016-01–05.

Sandoz, Ellis ed., *Political Sermons of the American Founding Era, 1730–1805*, vol. 1 (Indianapolis: Liberty Fund, 1998).

Schumacher, E.F., *Small is Beautiful* (New York: Harper Perennial, 1973).

Schwab, Klaus, "Now is the Time for a Great Reset," *World Economic Forum*, June 3, 2020. https://www.weforum.org/agenda/2020/06/now-is-the-time-for-a-great-reset/.

Shatz, Sanford and Ramey, Shaun, *American Bar Association- Business Law Section*, Sept. 14, 2021. https://businesslawtoday.org/2021/09/supreme-court-strikes-down-the-cdcs-second-eviction-moratorium/.

Silverstein, Jake, "The 1619 Project: Introduction," *The New York Times Magazine*, Aug. 18, 2019, pg. 4.

Smith, Adam, *Wealth of Nations*, vol. I and II (Indianapolis: Liberty Fund, 1981).

Smithsonian Institution Museum of African American History and Culture, "Whiteness." https://nmaahc.si.edu/learn/talking-about-race/topics/whiteness.

Sommeiller, Estelle and Price, Mark, "The New Gilded Age," *Economic Policy Institute*, July 19, 2018. https://www.epi.org/publication/the-new-gilded-age-income-inequality-in-the-u-s-by-state-metropolitan-area-and-county/

Sprint. "I am Unlimited," Jan. 31, 2013. https://www.youtube.com/watch?v=GCUO3-yq3eg.

Stack, Jack, *A Stake in the Outcome* (New York: Currency Books, 2002).

Stegner, Wallace, *Where the Bluebird Sings to the Lemonade Springs* (New York: Modern Library, 1992).

Stewart Emily, "Rep. Jim Clyburn Has Been Here Before," *Vox*, June 16, 2020. https://www.vox.com/policy-and-politics/2020/6/16/21289697/jim-clyburn-charleston-church-shooting-anniversary-protests-defund-police.

Storing, Herbert J. ed., *The Anti-Federalist*, (Chicago: University of Chicago Press, 1981).

Tocqueville, Alexis de, *Democracy in America*, translated and edited by Harvey C. Mansfield and Delba Winthrop (Chicago: The University of Chicago Press, 2000).

United States Congress (116th), H. Res. 109. https://www.congress.gov/bill/116th-congress/house-resolution/109/text.

United States Supreme Court. Department of Commerce v. New York. https://supreme.justia.com/cases/federal/us/588/18–966/.

Veith, Gene Edward, Jr., *God at Work* (Wheaton, IL: Crossway, 2011).

Warren, Elizabeth, "A Plan for Economic Patriotism," June 4, 2019. https://medium.com/@teamwarren/a-plan-for-economic-patriotism-13b879f4cfc7.

Weaver, Richard, *Ideas Have Consequences* (Chicago: University of Chicago Press, 1948).

World Economic Forum, "Our Partners." https://www.weforum.org/partners.

——— "You'll Own Nothing and You'll be Happy," https://www.dailymotion.com/video/x7y4pxt.

Wu, Nicholas, "Tucker Carlson on Elizabeth Warren: 'She Sounds Like Donald Trump at His Best,' *USA Today*, June 6, 2019. https://www.usatoday.com/story/news/politics/onpolitics/2019/06/06/tucker-carlson-praises-elizabeth-warren-trump-his-best/1364252001/.

Younis, Mohamed, "4 in Ten Americans Embrace Some Form of Socialism," *Gallup News*, May 20. 2019. https://news.gallup.com/poll/257639/four-americans-embrace-form-socialism.aspx.

Index

A

abortion, 118–19, 129
Abraham, 21
absolute ownership, 120
Adam and Eve, 20
Adams, John, 44–45
Amazon, 69, 99, 138, 147
American Dream, 10, 141
Anti-Federalists, 55–56
Aquinas, St. Thomas, 24, 121–22
Aristotle, 19–20, 78–79, 110–11
Articles of Confederation, 47
Augustine, 79–80
Auken, Ida, 148

B

Belloc, Hilaire, 98
Biden, Joe, 3, 12, 147, 149
Big Business, x, 11, 13–14
Big Government, x, 10–11, 13, 14, 68
Black Lives Matter, 149–52
BlackRock, 69, 138, 147
Bloomberg, Michael, 92–93
Burke, Edmund, 64

C

Cain and Abel, 20–21
Chesterton, G.K., 98–99
citizenship, 53, 105–110, 119, 127,
    134, 137–38, 142, 153
climate change, x, xiv, 2, 4, 9, 30, 97,
    98, 120, 124–25
Clinton, Hillary, 11

Clyburn, Jim, 3
communism, 5
coronavirus, 2–3, 4, 7, 9, 12, 98, 117,
    133, 146

D

Declaration of Independence, 25–26,
    45–46
Declaratory Act, 41–42
Democratic Party, 1, 2, 3, 12, 13, 14,
    91, 93, 96, 97, 149
Democratic Socialists of America, 95
Descartes, René, 19
Downer, Silas, 42–43

E

Edwards, John, 91
Employee Stock Ownership Plans,
    137
Enclosure Movement, 66
envy, 8
equality, 8, 31, 41, 52–54, 58, 59–60,
    63–64, 66, 69, 109, 131, 134, 139
Essex Report, 47–48

F

Facebook, 99, 138, 147
Federalist Papers, ix, 49–51
Floyd, George, 3–4, 6, 150–51
French Revolution, 65–66

G

Galsworthy, John, "Quality", 74–75
general will, 64–65
Glorious Revolution, 38–39
Google, 69, 99, 138
Gracchi brothers, 130–31
Great Reset, 146–48, 152
Green New Deal, 2, 6, 95, 101, 102,
    108, 148, 152

H

habit, 110–11
Hamilton, Alexander, 49
hate speech, 9
Hayek, F.A., 99
holidays, 77
Homer, *Iliad*, 19
Homestead Act of 1862, 29
Hopkins, Stephen, 39–40

I

immigration, 105, 127
inequality, xiii, 5, 7, 9, 15, 23, 44,
    53–55, 57–58, 63, 72, 92, 94, 109,
    140, 142, 148
industrial aristocracy, 72
industrial revolution, 27, 66–69

J

Jamestown, 32–3
Jefferson, Thomas, 25, 29, 45, 56–58,
    73, 106, 107, 132, 138, 140, 152
Jesus Christ, 23, 112

K

Kavanaugh, Brett, 12
Kendi, Ibram X., 4, 150
Kerry, John, 147
Keynes, John Maynard, 103–4
kleptocracy, 108
Koch, Charles, 90–91

L

land, 18, 29, 34–35, 38–39, 42–43, 45,
    52, 57–58, 66, 85–86, 130, 132
liberal education, 127–28
limits, 53, 111, 119–20, 124
Locke, John, 24–26, 39, 58, 107, 118,
    121
looting, 4
Luther, Martin, 80–81

M

Madison, James, ix, x, 18, 49, 50–51,
    54, 56–58, 65, 138, 140
Magna Carta, 35–37, 38
Marx, Karl, xiii, 5–6, 14, 27–28,
    67–69, 71, 82–83, 85, 134, 137
Mason, Paul, 4,
Mather, Moses, 43–44
Mayflower Compact, 34
Micah (prophet), 21–22
middle class, x, xi, xiv, 2, 14–15,
    58–59, 68, 70, 93–94, 135, 140,
    144, 151–53
middle class virtues, 70, 113, 122,
    144, 151
Mises, Ludwig von, 86n.19
Montesquieu, 51–54, 113, 140
Mosaic Law, 21

N

New Deal, 29–30, 101
New Testament Church, 23
New York Times, "1619 Project", 150
noblesse oblige, 109, 141

O

Obama, Barak, 30
Ocasio-Cortez, Alexandra, 2, 3, 97
Occupy Wall Street, 11, 92–93, 96
original sin, 65

P

Penn, William, 37–38
Petition of Right, 36–37

Plato, 22–23, 119, 140
Plutarch, 131
plutocracy, x-xiii, 11, 13, 15, 73, 98,
    108–110, 114, 134, 139, 147, 148
plutocratic socialism, xii–xiv, 14,
    59, 62, 109, 114, 133, 134, 142,
    147–48
police, 88–89, 140–41
privacy, 115–19
proprietas oblige, 142
protest, 96–97
public policy, 136–42

R

racism, 4–5, 150–51
Republican Party, 3, 13, 14, 91, 94, 96,
    100, 149
revolution, xiii–xiv, 5, 6, 14, 28, 69,
    70, 80, 134, 139, 150–52
riots, 150–52
Roe v. Wade, 118
Roosevelt, Franklin, 101–2
Röpke, Wilhelm, 73, 85, 86, 87,
    1x42n5
Rousseau, Jean Jacques, 62–66

S

sabbath, 76–77
Sanders, Bernie, 2, 11, 90, 91, 95, 97
scale and property, 138–39
Schumacher, E.F., 84
Sermon on the Mount, 23
sex, 116, 129
slavery, 26
Smith, Adam, 26–27, 83
socialism, xiii, 1–3, 5–6, 9–11, 15,
    29, 59, 69, 95, 98–99, 101, 134,
    141–42

St. Paul, 79
Stamp Act, 40–41
Stegner, Wallace, 34–35
stewardship, 18, 120–29, 135–36

T

Tea Party, 10
Tocqueville, Alexis de, 8, 14, 69–72,
    81–82, 101, 107, 152
tolerance, 9
"too big to fail", 92
Trump, Donald, 11, 94–96, 147, 149

U

United States Constitution, ix, x, 14,
    48, 49, 54, 55
U.S. Constitutional Order, x, 15, 131,
    134, 135, 141, 143, 145, 148

V

value and property, 85–86, 99
virtue, 104–10, 110–14
vocation, 80–81

W

Warren, Elizabeth, 93–95, 97
Weaver, Richard, 83–84
Webster, Noah, 54–55
welfare state, xi, xiii, 5, 14, 15, 30, 68,
    69, 87–88, 138, 140, 153
woke capital, xii
woke socialism, xii, 2, 5–6, 9–10, 15,
    31 59, 97, 104, 108, 119, 134,
    144, 148
World Economic Forum, 30, 146–48

www.ingramcontent.com/pod-product-compliance
Lightning Source LLC
Chambersburg PA
CBHW030848270326
41928CB00008B/1277